What Happens When Women Pray

VICTOR BOOKS BY EVELYN CHRISTENSON

What Happens When Women Pray

EVELYN CHRISTENSON

with Viola Blake

ChariotVICTOR

◆ P U B L I S H I N G ◆

A DIVISION OF COOK COMMUNICATIONS

Cassette and video tapes of Evelyn Christenson's seminars are
available. For more information write Evelyn Christenson Ministries,
4265 Brigadoon Dr., St. Paul, MN 55126

Unless otherwise noted, Scripture quotations are from the
Authorized (King James) Version of the Bible. Other quotations are
from The Living Bible (TLB), 1971, Tyndale House Publishers,
Wheaton, Illinois 60189.

Cover Design: Bill Gray
Cover Illustration: Barbara Rhodes

Library of Congress Cataloging-in-Publication Data

Christenson, Evelyn.
  What happens when women pray / Evelyn Christenson.
     p.   cm.
  ISBN 1-5647-6630-6
  1. Prayer, 2. Christenson, Evelyn. I. Title.
BV210.2.C53   1992
248.3'2'082–dc20   91-30779
                                            CIP

Victor Books is an imprint of ChariotVictor Publishing,
a division of Cook Communications, Colorado Springs, Colorado
80918. Cook Communications, Paris, Ontario
Kingsway Communications, Eastbourne, England

Deluxe edition, First Printing 1997

5 4 3   Printing/Year 01 00 99 98

DEDICATION

I am deeply grateful to the two Jims of Victor Books whose vision and expertise made this book possible and produced my round-the-world prayer ministry.

TO JIM LEMON

who was the first to recognize the need for this type of teaching on prayer, and who then stepped out in faith and marketed it to the Christian world.

TO JIM ADAIR

who had enough confidence in the material on the prayer seminar tapes of an unknown to put it into book form, patiently teaching and encouraging me until a book was born.

Without them, this book never would have been written.

$\mathcal{W}$hen I was a little girl, my parents owned a greenhouse filled with blooming flowers. It was during the Depression, and when things got really difficult, we always knew where we could find my mother— standing praying in the calla lily bed. She was surrounded by tall, stately lilies, their pure white faces lifted toward heaven. Mother told me, "The calla lilies seem so pure and holy that I can almost feel them breathing up to God." So the calla lily became our family flower, reminding us of her prayers and ours.

Contents

PREFACE

So, what *did* happen when women prayed?

When I conducted the prayer experiment in 1968 that produced this book, the title was still a question: What *will* happen if women pray? But now, almost thirty years later, I no longer am asking that question. I know!

I had been asked by a large nationwide evangelism movement to do a prayer experiment with the women of my own church, Temple Baptist, of Rockford, Illinois. I was to find out in six months time exactly what *did* happen when women prayed. "No more theories," they said. "Just pray for someone, and then afterward ask and record what really did happen."

I panicked in the predawn blackness that first day of 1968. I didn't know *if* my women would pray with me, and, even worse, I didn't know *if* they prayed—*if* God would do anything. And I had just six months to find out!

But such exciting and life-changing results were experienced during those six months, from the actual daily praying and the methods of prayer we worked out, that I began sharing them at retreats, workshops, church meetings, and conventions from coast to coast and in Canada. They went from a committee of eight women complaining about why they were asked to seeing the worth of themselves in prayer—in just one month!

Now, almost thirty years later, I look back in awe as I see how God amazingly multiplied His original promise to us that *"the effectual, fervent prayer of a righteous person **avails much**"* (James 5:16b). For over twenty years there has been a steady stream of letters, calls, and readers in my autograph lines excitedly telling me how prayer changed their lives—as it had ours. Tens of thousands have accepted Jesus through it, marriages have been put back together, family relationships mended, even lives saved—by God—when THEY learned to pray.

After moving to Minnesota in late 1970 where my husband had joined the staff of Bethel College and Seminary, again it felt so dark. I had left the security and joy of churchwide prayer in my husband's pastorate. But one morning God sternly reminded me to stir up the gift that was in me. "What gift?" I numbly asked. "The gift of prayer, of course!" He retorted. So I began launching Bible studies on prayer, which turned into five- or six-week interdenominational prayer seminars with over 100,000 learning to pray in them. Soon it became necessary to consolidate all the material into one-day seminars of six intensive hours as invitations flowed in unsolicited from other states and Canada. Then we launched our now twenty years of broadcasting from the book, reaching over one-half of the world's population with thrilling responses of prayer where many had never even heard the name of Jesus.

Having learned so thoroughly that it is God, not plans and programs, that "avail much," I had immediately organized an advisory/prayer board. As about thirty ordinary women started meeting monthly, praying daily, organizing twenty-four hour prayer clocks, and operating our still-running telephone prayer chains, God immediately began to show me what He would do if *they* prayed. We incorporated in 1973, and United Prayer Ministry was born. To this day they have prayed through every open door, success, and stumbling block of the ministry. Every word of this book, and all my books and teachings, have been fervently prayed through by them—plus by personal prayer support groups, the Bethel College faculty women, and family members.

Years later I would discover that God had been mustering a whole army of women to pray in the early 1970s—and we were part of it. Campus Crusade's Great Commission Prayer Crusade, Aglow, Lydia, and numerous other groups were rapidly expanding by the thousands—praying for our country's leaders, their churches, pastors, schools, children, and husbands. Today we are part of the greatest worldwide prayer movement that Christianity has ever known.

From 1968 to 1974 people in seminars would ask, "Is this material in print?" My answer was always the same. "God has not told me it should be in print. *You* pray if you think it should be. If God wants this in a book, He will open the doors." And so they prayed.

God did miraculously open the publishing door to a very surprised future author. Jim Lemon, the vice president of marketing for Victor Books and a friend through Bethel College, was riding in our car and casually asked what I was doing those days. I said I was teaching interdenominational prayer seminars, and he asked if they were on tape. Embarrassed, I admitted I had a suitcase full of the tapes we were selling in the back seat of the car. He took a set, had Jim Adair and the editorial staff of Victor Books listen to the whole six hours of teaching, called me, and said, "You have a contract." "A what?" I stammered. "A contract for a book. Get yourself an editor who can help arrange your spoken words into book form. We like your material." So we transcribed the entire taped seminar, and Viola Blake, the then assistant editor of Billy Graham's *Decision Magazine*, supervised writing them down.

But the amazing thing was *God's timing* for a book on prayer. Had it been published earlier, our women would not have been ready for it. But in 1975 when it came out, our country was seeking answers. The militant side of the women's lib movement was dividing our society and churches, we had become the ugly American overseas, and the Watergate scandal had eroded our trust in government. We needed an anchor. And prayer was that anchor.

After a few years my board made a new discovery in Jeremiah 33:3. God said: *"Call unto me AND I will answer, AND I will show you great and mighty things **you know not**."* We had prayed and God had answered. (We had books full of dated requests and answers to prove it.) But suddenly we saw that God was doing the *last* part of that promise—revealing amazing things we never had asked for or even thought of—just because we prayed!

Without our being aware of it, God was the book's distributor. There never has been a universal, or even a national, advertising program for it, yet it is literally all over the world. I have ministered on every continent, but this book always has preceded me. In every foreign country, I have been surprised to find people already studying and praying with it. I was shocked to find its telephone prayer chains operational in churches, entire cities, and even whole nations. Bible studies and Sunday school classes everywhere are still studying its prerequisites to answered prayer. There never has been a request for a meeting from us. God has opened doors to virtually all denominations, hundreds of organizations, and the world.

When Victor Books celebrated the book's one millionth copy, they asked me to speak in chapel on what produces a million-copy book. My answer was simply, "Well, prayer, of course." It is about prayer, an actual prayer experiment produced it, every single word in that book, every production problem, even the truck strike delivering the paper were prayed for. And an assigned Prayer Calendar intercessor has prayed for its use every day since.

Now, having sold over two million copies in America, plus being printed all around the world, my heart goes back in humble gratitude and awe to God who promised us in 1968 that *the effectual, fervent **prayer** of a righteous person avails much.* Not our clever plans, advertising programs, persuasive presentations of the material—but God answering prayer!

However, in spite of the ever-growing corporate praying, my own personal prayer life has been the essential basis of it all. Lessons I have taught through the years all came directly from God. It has taken a minimum of two hours a day alone with God, basically in the pre-dawn hours of the night, interacting with Him over every step of this journey. Weeping over my sins . . . pleading for His wisdom . . . overwhelmed as He lavishly bestowed it . . . silently enfolded in His arms, sometimes for hours, just loving Him and feeling His love for me . . . sometimes resisting Satan who is terrified over a saint on his or her knees . . . sometimes bursting with praise and thanksgiving—awestruck at what He is doing.

At seventy-five years of age I look back with awe at what God has done—and stand almost breathless at what He wants to do.

My generation mostly has passed the torch to the next generation of sharp, well-educated leaders. But what is even more exciting to me is the next generation in their twenties and early thirties—emerging dissatisfied with what they were handed by most of us—eager, almost desperate, to find answers from God for themselves and their families to the ever-eroding values and escalating evil in our country.

Today, are you searching for an anchor? In whatever age group you find yourself, there is one. I know! Plug into the power of the omnipotent God of Heaven through prayer—and hang on! Only He has an inkling of the great and mighty things He has in store for you—when YOU pray.

Evelyn Christenson
St. Paul, Minnesota
April, 1997

Prayer Is the Answer

The effectual fervent prayer of a righteous (person) availeth much. James 5:16

ord, help! How do I motivate eight gripers?"
Here they were, on a cold January morning, sitting around my dining room table—the favored ones, those who had been chosen to learn to pray. I thought they would be enthusiastic about the idea. Weren't they all Spiritual Life Chairmen of women's circles at church? Instead, they sat there griping.

Earlier, in the fall of 1967, the national committee of our denomination had asked me to do a project for the Crusade of the Americas. "Working with women in your own church, would you discover in a six-month period what happens when women pray?"

I had replied, "I'll take that task."

It had sounded so simple in 1967. But on New Year's morning I awakened with a jolt: "It's 1968, and I have to find out what happens when women pray!" I didn't have a single thought in my head. I didn't know how to start. I didn't know with whom I should start. What would you have done? I panicked.

But as I was lying there I said, "Lord, please help. I feel negative. Everything is black. It's dark and it's cold and it's everything it shouldn't be. What shall I do? Show me."

Suddenly, just as if a horizontal door opened over my head, God was speaking to me, though there was no audible voice. He said, "Evelyn, if you're going to find out what happens when women pray, you are going to have to learn to use this door, the door of access to Me. This is the door of prayer. You, Evelyn, are going to have to learn to use it more effectively."

I simply said, "Thank You, Lord. Now I know just what to do."

That week I called together those eight spiritual life chairmen of the women's circles in the church where my husband was pastor. I thought, "This will really do it. These women will all be excited about learning to pray; they will be the steering committee."

Instead they griped. "I'm the spiritual life chairman of my circle," one said, "but all the president lets me do is close in prayer."

Another remarked, "My president lets me pray for the food, and that's it."

They went on and on. Evidently they didn't know what I was talking about. That's when I silently cried to the Lord for help. He answered, "Evelyn, back way up and tell them about yourself."

"You know," I began, "I want to tell you something about your pastor's wife. I never teach a Sunday School class, never lead my neighborhood Bible study, never speak anywhere, without calling on my two strong prayer partners. The three of us pray earnestly that God will enable me to speak."

"Not you," they said. "Not our pastor's wife. You don't have any needs."

"Your pastor's wife needs prayer," I insisted; "she knows very well that she can fall flat on her face if there isn't prayer support."

I still wasn't getting through to these eight women. I had to back up some more. "In 1961, six months after I had major surgery, I was scheduled to speak at just one session of a retreat. I thought that after six months I'd be flying high, but I wasn't. A series of infections had slowed my recovery. From that standpoint, to accept the engagement was a foolish thing for me to do, but after making me comfortable in the car, my husband drove me to the conference grounds.

"All during the dinner hour I didn't say a word, I know that if I talked then, I wouldn't have enough strength to address the ladies afterward. By 10 P.M. I still hadn't been called on to speak—you know how women's retreats go on and on. Weak and trembling I searched out the chairwoman and said, 'Joyce, forget the whole thing. I don't have enough strength left to speak. I can't say one word.'

"Joyce Ankerberg replied, 'Just a minute, Evelyn.' She went to summon a very mature 'prayer' whom she knew. The three of us found a little room with bunks in it, and we got down on our knees. Those two women prayed until I had enough strength to go out there and speak. At the end of the meeting we had a fireside service of rededication, and only 10 of the 400 women present did not rededicate their lives to Christ."

I had at last convinced my eight women that their pastor's wife depended 100 percent on prayer when she went out to minister for Christ. Slowly, they began to pray.

"O Lord, show me."

"Lord, cleanse me."

"Lord, use me." That was all they prayed that first time, but it was a beginning.

CONVERSION AT THE COUNTRY CLUB

Gradually, as they learned simple methods of praying effectively, God began to encourage these former gripers with beautiful answers to prayer. The first exciting result was a dramatic conversion. I had been teaching a weekly neighborhood Bible study specifically designed to introduce women to Christ, but nothing was happening. I said to the eight women, who were now praying every Tuesday morning, "I have a problem. Let's zero in on one person in that Bible study group. I know that Marion doesn't know Christ as her personal Savior." That morning we prayed, and we prayed.

Then I told them, "I'm taking Marion to lunch." Right away they volunteered to pray while we were at lunch, and through the afternoon. As they were leaving, one said, "I'm going to pray that you take her to a place where you can really talk."

Each woman took a similar specific request home with her, and I drove on to Marion's house. When I got there she said, "Let me drive." So with my little Bible under my arm I got into her big white Cadillac convertible and we drove to her country club. Have you ever led anyone to the Lord in a country club? I hadn't, and I wasn't at all sure what was going to happen next.

Since Marion's husband owned much of the stock in that country club, the host bowed and scraped and asked, "Wouldn't you like this nice secluded table here in the corner?" It was just the right spot for conversation. We talked and talked while the waitress kept bringing us coffee. I finally said, "You know, Marion, I think it's time we stop talking and go out to the car and pray."

What had we been talking about all afternoon? Marion had been picking my brains about Jesus. "How do you accept Jesus into your life? What is it like to have Jesus in your heart? What's it like living with Him?" So many questions. But at 3:20 Marion jumped up and together we went out to the parking lot, sat in that big white Cadillac, and Marion bowed her head and prayed, "O God, forgive all my sins; and Jesus, please come in to be my Savior." Marion had found Christ.

Another exciting part of this story unfolded on the following Thursday morning when the dear woman who helped me clean once a week opened my front door with the immediate question, "What happened on Tuesday?"

"Why, Mary, what do you mean, 'What happened on Tuesday?' "

She explained, "Well, the Lord said on Sunday, 'Now, Mary, you fast and pray,' so I didn't eat; I just prayed from Sunday until Tuesday afternoon. Then in the middle of the afternoon the Lord said to me, 'It's okay, Mary, you can eat now.' What happened on Tuesday afternoon?"

I said, "Mary, would you believe that at 3:20 on Tuesday afternoon Marion accepted Christ?"

Mary was huge, and she put those big arms around me, and I put my arms almost around Mary, and we stood there and cried, for she and I had prayed together for Marion by name for many months.

PRAYERS, NOT PLANS OR PROGRAMS

We learned that things could happen when we didn't plan at all but just prayed. A long distance call came to our church after one of the Sunday morning services. It was Arthur Blessit calling from California. "May I use your church building for a meeting on Tuesday night?" he asked. "You won't have to do a thing. I just want to reach some hippies for Christ."

My husband said, "Fine, you may use our church."

Arthur arrived on Tuesday morning. There had been no time to advertise the meeting in local newspapers or in other churches. The only means of communication had been the hippie "underground" method. But Tuesday morning was our prayer time. The entire kitchen area of the church was "wall to wall" with women who had only one prayer—that somehow the hippies of the area would hear there was to be a meeting for them in our church that night.

As we were praying, our church secretary. Carolyn, came flying downstairs and interrupted our prayer with, "The religion editor of our newspaper came to interview Art Blessit; now they're on their knees praying!" The religion editor received Christ. Art Blessit's meeting had front-page coverage that evening. How else would you get newspaper advertising in such short time?

We had 1,100 hippies in our church that night. They had come from as far away as Chicago—ninety miles—by thumb, by motorcycle, by car. Some were on hard drugs. These characters, and I mean characters, came en masse to the service. When Art gave the invitation that night over 100 of them accepted Christ. As the Christians came forward to find a place to pray with these young people, there wasn't a closet, or a hallway, or a side room anywhere in the church where people weren't already praying!

My husband is a very organized man. In fact, he is now teaching a course in management in a seminary. But the next Sunday he laid aside his already prepared sermon and announced, "I can speak on only one subject this morning: 'What Happens When You Don't Plan, You Just Pray!' "

PRAY FIRST, PLAN AFTERWARD

God expects us to be orderly. He expects us to manage our time, to discipline ourselves, to prepare well-planned programs, but if we could learn to pray first and plan afterward, how different would be our homes, our churches, our Christian women's club, our Bible studies, whatever we are doing for Christ. Maybe, just maybe, we are planning in one direction and God's will is in another direction. God might say, "Hold everything! Turn around and go this way. This is My will for you, not that way."

Even if we are plugged into God's will and know we're going in the right direction, we may be going at a snail's pace. God says, "Look, you see only a tenth of what I have for you. There are nine-tenths that you're not seeing, that you don't know anything about."

God wants us to make ourselves available to Him, and to say before we start to plan, "Lord, tell me what You want me to do, where You want me to go, how you want me to do it." Then our omnipotent God, with all the abundance of heaven at His disposal, will pour out His power upon us. Instead of following our tiny, tiny plans, God wants to open heaven and flood us. It's exciting.

In our early days of learning to pray, the best source of requests was the Christian Education department of our church. Gail, our children's worker, came up with a fantastic idea after she witnessed some miraculous answers to prayer. Her suggestion, "Let's pray first and plan afterward," became the slogan for our church. During Vacation Bible School that year we set up a prayer room and collected requests along with attendance sheets. Then teachers and helpers spent their break times in prayer.

An urgent request came from one department. Not one child had received Christ, though the school had been in session for a week and a half. That Wednesday morning we zeroed in on that request. The same teacher was giving the same kind of Bible story, but what a difference prayer made. I stepped into the department to see twenty-three hands raised to receive Christ. The spiritual ceiling of our church went straight up!

NO DRY EYES

The original notes I made for my report at our national conference in 1968 reveal what happened in six months as we were learning to pray:

January—the gripe session. "Cleanse me. . . . Use me. . . . Forgive me. . . . Show me." That was all.

February—eagerness had replaced complaining. They were excited. They were actually seeing the worth of themselves in prayer.

March—great joy and much sharing of answered prayer. They were talking about changes in their own lives due to praying.

April—there were no dry eyes as we were experientially learning what effectual, fervent prayer really is.

May—we were claiming victory over Satan as our specific prayers were answered in specific ways. We were learning that Satan gets busy when we actually pray, not when we study about prayer or even memorize Bible verses about prayer. But the exciting thing is that in prayer we gain victory over Satan.

June—by popular demand we opened our prayer meetings to all of our church women. In just six months we had learned that "the effectual, fervent prayer" of a righteous person avails much—not plans or programs, but effectual, fervent *prayer*.

An occult high priest was quoted in our local newspaper as saying that the churches of America have given up the supernatural. They don't deal in the supernatural; they just deal in plans and programs and social action. He said that every human being is created with a supernatural vacuum, and since Christians aren't doing anything in the realm of the supernatural, he feels that witchcraft is a reasonable substitute for Christianity.

Can we still have the supernatural in our churches? I think we can, for effectual, fervent prayer is capable of producing supernatural results.

The women of a 4,000-member church learned this in a two-session prayer seminar. A week later the wife of one of the four pastors told me, "The most amazing thing happened when we learned to pray: the Holy Spirit just went 'whoosh' through our church! I didn't tell you before, but we were just about to split. Our Christian Education department was deteriorating Sunday by Sunday, and members were pulling out. When nothing else worked, we decided to try prayer. Problems were solved and walls between the factions started to crumble."

I met her a year later and asked, "How is it going in your church?"

Her answer, "It's still going great."

UNITY IN THE COMMUNITY

The "availeth much" of prayer was apparent, but there was more to come. One of the surprises was the terrific unity we found in communities where members of the body of Christ learned to pray together. *Caution:* This refers to the body of Christ praying together, not just church members.

Last year I met the pastor of the host church where our first prayer seminar was held. He said to me, "Ev, you know our daughter was killed in a tragic accident last month, and an amazing thing happened at her funeral. There were priests and pastors and lay people from every single church in the area." And then he added, "This never would have happened if the women had not learned to pray together."

Was it because they met for a series of six meetings? No. It was because they had learned the unifying dimension of prayer.

Marcella, wife of the mayor of a northern Minnesota town, had a fantastic vision of what God could do when women prayed. One day she called and said, "Evelyn, I'm concerned about our town. There are lots of Christians here, but we all go our own directions. We compete rather than work together for the cause of Christ. Could you come for a rally?"

One of the miracles at that rally was that there were representatives from every single church present. After the meeting a woman came to me and said, "I'm chairman of the women's committee here, and I know why this rally was a success."

"Okay," I said, "you tell me."

"Well, Marcella told us last May, 'If Evelyn's coming for a rally, she expects you to be praying. Now get on the ball.' So we did and we have prayed in an organized fashion every other week from May to October."

I was still shaking hands with the women when a beautiful blond girl stepped up to me and asked, "Why am I here?"

I sort of blinked and replied, "Don't you know why you're here?"

"No, I don't know why I'm here. I've never been in this church before, but this afternoon a very peculiar thing happened to me. All at once it was if an irresistible force was urging me to come to this meeting tonight; I thought I'd better come. Why am I here?"

I looked at her and asked, "Honey, do you know Christ as your Savior?"

She replied, "No, I don't."

Then I asked, "Would you like to?"

She said, "Yes, I would like to."

After I finished shaking hands we went downstairs and prayed together, and there she accepted Christ as her personal Savior.

Marcella envisioned something more for the Christian women of her town—a retreat. Several months later the women who had begun to feel their marvelous unity in Christ came to the retreat. One was the same little blond I had prayed with before. "I now know what that irresistible force was," she said. "It was God's power. My husband has been a Christian for many years, and God has been calling him into full-time service, but I wasn't even a Christian. Now I'm going to be a pastor's wife. My husband has enrolled in seminary. What a horrible pastor's wife I would have made, not even knowing Jesus as my Savior."

As we were leaving the retreat one woman remarked to me, "I think we ought to call this the 'red-nose session.' Just look around at all the tears and all the red noses!" It was true. Women who formerly had crossed the street to keep from speaking to each other were now throbbing in one accord, in unity, loving each other in Christ. Something really happened there. An irresistible force had been at work, as a result of prayer.

One day my husband walked out of the sanctuary of our church and encountered our custodian fairly dripping with perspiration. He was a giant of a Christian, but was gradually losing his ability to think and work effectively because of hardening of the arteries. As my husband saw him struggling with the vacuum cleaner he looked down, and there lying on the floor was the plug. The dear man had vacuumed the whole auditorium and didn't have the plug in the outlet!

Isn't that what happens to many of us? We work, we pull, we struggle, and we plan until we're utterly exhausted, but we have forgotten to plug into the source of power. And that source of power is prayer—the "effectual, fervent prayer" of a righteous person that avails much.

For you to pray:

Dear God, teach me to plug into your power. Amen.

IT DOESN'T TAKE SO LONG

If I regard iniquity in my heart,
the Lord will not hear me. Psalm 66:18

ow's it going, Mrs. Chris?" My very good friend, Steve, one of our church boys, always asked me that question when he came home for an occasional weekend from Harvard School of Business.

Some days I answered, "Oh, it is going great. We just learned this kind of prayer and look what's happening. It's going just great!"

Then, when he would come home other times and ask how things were going, I would have a different answer. "Oh, did we fall on our faces this week! It was a mess. I don't know who suggested the method of prayer we tried this time, but it sure didn't work."

Finally Steve, with his youthful fervor, was getting a little exasperated hearing of the struggles we were having as we were learning to pray effectively. I'll never forget the day he and I met down by the piano in the front of the sanctuary. He stood there with his hands on his hips, and looking straight at me, asked, *"Mrs. Chris, why does it take so long?"*

I said, "Steve, I don't know. I wish I did. I'm sure it's not God's fault. This is all experimentation; it's trial and error for us. We're just learning. I really don't know why it's taking us so long."

Steve became a vice-president of an international Christian organization, and while he was teaching a management course in Atlanta, I sent him a message via one of our officers. I asked her to please tell Steve, "It doesn't take so long anymore."

Several weeks later when Steve visited us at our cottage on the shores of Lake Michigan, he said, "You know, when Jan gave me your message, 'It doesn't take so long anymore,' I had to scratch my head and wonder, *'What is Ev saying to me?'* Then I remembered my question back in 1968."

As I stood cooking the breakfast eggs in the cottage kitchen the next morning, I explained to Steve how and why it doesn't take so long anymore. It went something like the following.

EFFECTIVE FERVENT PRAYER
IN ONLY SIX WEEKS

Our first prayer seminar was held in White Bear Lake, Minnesota with twenty different churches represented. It was a six-week seminar, and the women were practicing simple, sometimes hesitant, audible praying. At the fifth session, one of the women shared with us that the occult had been invited into a local high school. Witches, with all their garb and paraphernalia, were instructing the students, including her daughter, in the ways of witchcraft. Of the 250 women present, many had children in that high school.

Fervent prayer really began then for those students and their teachers. In fact, women were praying so earnestly in their groups that I had to step to the microphone and tell them to conclude their praying because the baby-sitters had to go home! God had given them an urgent reason for learning to pray quickly.

God also gave them answers to their prayers. A group of Christian parents went to school officials about the matter and, as a result, Christian speakers were given equal time to expose the errors of the occult.

Something else was stirring in that first prayer seminar. It came from a group of women from a Catholic church who sat in the second row. I could always count on them to be in the same place each week. What an inspiration they were. At the third session one of them came to me and said, "Mrs. Christenson, we want you to know that after just two weeks of praying we are already in 'April praying.'"

I had to scratch my head and think, "April praying? April praying?" Oh, yes, I recalled having told the group that in 1968 it had taken us from January to April to get to our "no dry eyes," as we were experientially learning what effectual, fervent prayer really was. I said, "Tell me about your 'April praying.'"

She went on, "After the very first session, all of us from our church went home, and we promised each other that although we couldn't meet together every single day, we would pray for our church every morning at 9 o'clock. In just two weeks we are seeing fantastic things happen; we are already in 'April praying.'"

A couple of weeks later they brought me a copy

of their church bulletin. One of the women said, "Look what our priest has written!"

I read, "If all these wonderful things happen to women who learn to pray, let's start praying as families."

The priest even began to preach a series of sermons on prayer because that little group practiced what they had learned the very first week.

This is what's exciting to me about the prayer seminars. There is always a nucleus of people, both men and women from all denominations, going back and turning their churches upside down.

I said to Steve, "It took only two weeks for the group from that church to learn to pray. No, it doesn't take so long anymore."

SIX MONTHS, SIX WEEKS, SIX HOURS

One day a district leader of the Young Life Campaigners came to me with a question, "Do you think you could teach our Campaigners to pray in six hours? We're planning to meet at a college, but there's going to be a wedding there at 7 o'clock, so we have to be out of the building by 3."

I blinked, and thought, "Six hours! Six weeks is one thing; six months is how long it took us at first, but now this group is asking for only six hours!" I said, "I don't know if I can, but I'll try."

We met together at 9 o'clock in the morning. By 11 A.M. those teenagers, many of whom were disenchanted with the established church, had pushed back their chairs and were kneeling on the floor, fervently praying in little circles. I felt tears spring to my eyes at that sight—after only two hours.

Recently, in Fargo, North Dakota we had our first one day seminar. I had to tell the ladies that I wasn't sure it would work, but we plunged in, breaking just once for midmorning coffee. Then, following lunch, we had an all-afternoon session. At the end of the day, the chairman said to me, "Evelyn, the most exciting thing to me has been to hear this fervent prayer so soon by 100 percent of the people who have just learned to pray today." How long does it take? It doesn't take so long.

RELEASED TO PRAY FOR OTHERS

I want to share with you one other six-week session that took place in the fall on 1964 when my two prayer partners, Lorna and Signe, and I began to pray together. Everything seemed to be going great in our church. In four years our membership had almost doubled, a building program was in progress, and we had a full schedule of activities to meet the needs of our congregation. Yet, the three of us sensed that there was a missing dimension. We decided to meet once a week to pray for our church—a very noble idea, we thought.

We agreed at the start to base our praying on a verse of Scripture—a good rule to follow—and right away God gave us Psalm 66:18: "If I regard iniquity in my heart, the Lord will not hear me."

"Lord, what do You mean?" we asked. "We're going to pray for our church." But He continued to apply the pressure gently: "If *I* regard iniquity in *my* heart, the Lord will not hear me." Wow! I, the pastor's wife? Lorna and Signe? Uh huh.

God didn't release us to pray for other needs until we had cleaned up our own lives by confessing *our* sins. It took us, oh, so long. We prayed and prayed, and God kept bringing sins and sins to our minds. As our first prayer meeting came to a close, we thought, *"Phew! We got that one over with; next week we can start praying for the needs of the church."* But when we met the following week, we still couldn't get beyond Psalm 66:18! This was a new concept to us. God kept bringing our wrong priorities, thoughts, reactions, and attitudes to our minds. It took the three of us six weeks—six whole weeks—to get out of Psalm 66:18 and into effectual, fervent praying. I see one of those prayer partners occasionally, and we still shake our heads at that one!

You don't have that many things to clean up in your life do you? But I did, as a pastor's wife. Someone once asked me, "What kinds of sins do pastors' wives commit, or is that too personal?"

Not knowing how to answer her offhand, I decided to compile a list from memory of the many sins we confessed then. Two days later Signe stopped in the Twin Cities en route back to her home from California. "Sig, what specific sins do you remember from those six weeks of Psalm 66:18 back in 1964?" I asked.

"The main one I remember," she replied immediately, "was our superior attitude concerning our spiritual status compared to others, and the idea that we should pray *for* them. God showed us that attitude was sin." (I added that one to the two-page list I had jotted down in answer to the question!)

What other sins had we confessed?

• Divided motives. All of us were very involved in serving Christ, thinking our reasons were all for His glory. But God showed us how much there was of ego, self-fulfillment, self-satisfaction, and desire to build up our own worth in the eyes of our fellow church members.

• Pretense. One said it was the first time in her life she was really honest before God. People had her on a spiritual pedestal; and she didn't dare admit even to her family, that she wasn't as spiritual as everybody told her she was. She also confessed to God a bad attitude toward one member of her family that no one could have dreamed was there.

• Pride. How surprised I was when God exposed as sin the feeling of "Look what I've done" that would come over me as I passed the mimeographed copies of *my* lesson outline to the members of my adult Sunday School class. I was never satisfied in the preparation of my lesson until I had exhausted the resources in my husband's library, put the volumes of notes in outline form, typed stencils, and run off copies for all.

None of us had been practicing the "dirty dozen" sins, but God exposed one by one the "little Christian sins" that Peter could have been referring to when he wrote, "For the eyes of the Lord are over the righteous, and His ears are open unto their prayers; but the face of the Lord is against them that do evil" (1 Peter 3:12).

A PREREQUISITE TO ANSWERED PRAYER

The three of us learned in a very practical way that there are prerequisites to effective intercessory prayer. There is one word we didn't touch on in the first chapter when we cited: "The effectual, fervent prayer of a righteous person availeth much." Did you catch what we missed? "The effectual fervent prayer" of what kind of person? A *righteous* person. It is his prayer, and only his, that availeth much. If we are living in sin and liking it, if we are keeping it there, finding that it feels kind of good, if we're regarding—nurturing, patting that little sin along— God does not hear us. The Prophet Isaiah gives a powerful description of someone in this plight:

> Listen now! The Lord isn't too weak to save you. And He isn't getting deaf! He can hear you when you call! But the trouble is that your sins have cut you off from God. Because of sin He has turned His face away from you and will not listen anymore (Isaiah 59:1-2, TLB).

Do you wonder why your prayers aren't answered? We're going to learn many reasons why they are not, in the chapters that follow, but here is the first one: sin (or sins) in your life. It is "the effectual, fervent prayer of a *righteous* person that availeth much." If your prayers aren't availing much, this may be the reason. Maybe it isn't. Maybe you're long past this. But I find that when I think I'm past this one, all at once a little pride pops up, and I have to confess it quickly, get it out, and then go on.

Your problem may not be *sins*, but *sin*. And this is a very important point. When our Lord was talking to His disciples just before His crucifixion, He told them that He was going to send the Comforter, the Holy Spirit, who would convict *the world*—those who were not Christ's followers—"of sin, because they believe not on Me" (John 16:9). *This is the sin that will keep God from hearing intercessory prayer—the sin of not believing in Christ as your personal Savior.* If this is your sin, the only prayer from you that God promises to hear is one of repentance and faith as you invite Christ into your life.

After we become Christians we commit *sins*. What do we do with them? Do we live with them? The answer is that we get rid of them. God gives Christians the formula: "If *we* confess *our* sins, He is faithful and just to forgive us *our sins*, and to cleanse us from all unrighteousness" (1 John 1:9). This is written only to Christians to tell us how we may be cleansed and ready for an effectual intercessory prayer life.

Even little sins can muddy up our communication system. We try to get through to God and there's something in the way. It may be an attitude, a spoken word. God wants these things cleared up. He doesn't want anything between Him and us. If there is, it's our fault, not His, when His ears are closed to our prayers.

Back in 1968, one dear woman objected to this. She said, "I don't like this one bit, this cleaning up of my life before I can be a good, strong, powerful intercessory pray-er."

Another countered, "Not me. I have preschool twin boys, and no matter how much I clean up my life before I start for this prayer meeting, by the time I reach here with them in the car, there's some attitude I have to get cleaned up before I can pray for others."

I found out later that the one who objected so strenuously was harboring a grave sin in her life. She didn't like this process, but it's very definite in God's Word. This, then, is the first prerequisite—nothing between God and ourselves when we approach intercessory prayer.

How long does it take? It really doesn't take so long.

For you to pray:

Dear Father, bring to my mind that sin or sins keeping You from hearing my intercessory prayers. I confess whatever You have brought to my mind as sin. Thank You, Lord, for cleansing me as You promised in 1 John 1:9 and qualifying me for effectual, intercessory prayer.

Forgiven as We Forgive

And forgive us our sins, just as we have forgiven those who have sinned against us. Matthew 6:12, TLB

ne horizontal dimension of prayer that Christ taught that is frequently overlooked by those seeking a deeper prayer life relates to the thing that is *most apt to break up your prayer group*—your relationship with the other people who are in that group!

In the Lord's Prayer we read, "And forgive us our sins just *as* we have forgiven those who have sinned against us" (Matthew 6:12, TLB). Your Bible translation may say debts or trespasses; both have the same literal meaning: *sins*. Now, this is the Lord Jesus Himself teaching the disciples, and us in turn, how to pray. If you want to keep your prayer group intact, practice this principle.

That word *as* is a conditional word meaning "to the extent that"—to the extent that I forgive others, I'm asking God to forgive me.

Christ explained it like this: "Your heavenly Father will forgive you if you forgive those who sin against you, but if you refuse to forgive them, He will not forgive you" (Matthew 6:14-15, TLB).

Do you remember our first prerequisite to answered prayer, in chapter 2, "If I regard iniquity in my heart, the Lord will not hear me"? (Psalm 66:18) Christ says that if we don't forgive others, our

Heavenly Father will not forgive us. If He does not, our sins will keep Him from hearing our intercessory prayers. They will be of no avail.

So, unless we keep our relationships with other people clear, we cannot be effective intercessory pray-ers. Now, let's remember one more thing from chapter 2: God always hears the penitent sinner's prayer confessing sin and seeking Christ as Savior. God also hears the plea for forgiveness of sins by the one who is already a Christian. But for us to refuse to forgive others is itself a sin. We can't be right with God and effective intercessors if we harbor the sin of an unforgiving spirit—even though we may have confessed all *other* known sins. This is a very difficult lesson for some to learn, but it is very important.

Jesus also admonished His disciples, in rather strong words, "Listen to Me! You can pray for anything, and if you believe, you have it; it's yours! But—when you are praying, first forgive anyone you are holding a grudge against, so that your Father in heaven will forgive you your sins too" (Mark 11: 24-25, TLB).

DEALING WITH THOSE WHO CAUSE GRIEF

I want to share with you the way this truth was brought into focus for me in the summer of 1972. I was all set to speak at a prayer breakfast for vacationers and women from several churches in Michigan. It was possible that some people present would not know Christ, so I first made a telephone call to the spiritual life chairman of a local prayer chain and gave her my request. She jotted it down, dated it, and indicated that she would be happy to take care of the whole thing. Still feeling the need for special prayer, I called another local chain and then dialed long distance back to my former prayer chain in Rockford for their support.

When I got back home, I called the prayer chains to send through praise for God's blessing at the prayer breakfast. The spiritual life chairman to whom I spoke during my first call was very quiet for a minute. Then she said, "Um, we didn't pray."

I exclaimed, "You didn't pray?"

"No," she replied, "one of the members said, 'We don't pray for speakers on this prayer chain.'"

I was stunned, and I gathered that this woman was seeing prayer needs only with her physical eyes, not with her spiritual eyes, for this was a spiritual need. The person who had enough authority to prevent a prayer from going through an entire prayer chain stopped it dead—and no one received the request.

How did I react? Just like a human being. I admit it was wrong, but I was very grieved for several days. And my spiritual life? I can only explain it by saying it became just like straw. If you want your prayer group to fall apart, to become like straw, just become grieved with another person, in the same way I did.

Soon after this incident, Chris and I took a vacation 9,000 feet up in the Rockies. It should have been a beautiful time of fellowship with God, but I couldn't get through to Him in prayer. My Bible reading was meaningless; my whole spiritual life still felt just like straw. I was grating away on the inside and feeling perfectly miserable.

Finally, by Thursday of that week, I had had it. At 5 A.M. I grabbed my Bible, went out under those gorgeous pine trees, knelt by an old pine log, and cried out to God, "Show me what's wrong with my life. I can't get through to You."

I leafed through the pages of my Bible, but God was silent. Then in desperation I turned another page, and my eyes fell on the words right at the bottom of a page, "If any have caused grief." *Why, Lord, that's what's wrong with me,* I thought. *I've been grieved.* Then God spoke to me, "Why don't you read on?" I read on and Wow! What I discovered was a *formula* to remedy my ailment.

I remember the exact page in my *King James Version*; it was page 1253 where God met me. This prescription was for me as an individual, and it's also for you as an individual, and for your prayer group as well. It will keep your prayer group and your prayer chain intact. The Scripture passage is 2 Corinthians 2:5-11.

"But if any have caused grief" (v. 5). Yes, this woman had caused me grief all right! Though I was innocent, I was still grieved—and miserable.

"Sufficient to such a person is this punishment, which was inflicted by the many" (v. 6). I suddenly realized that she was being shunned not only by me, but by others who had learned of her refusal to let my prayer request be put on the prayer chain. The news had gotten around.

"So that contrariwise ye ought rather to forgive" (v. 7). I saw that I had to forgive. You see, God wasn't

hearing my prayers. I had asked Him for forgiveness, but I hadn't forgiven the person who had grieved me. So I prayed, "Father, give me the strength to forgive this person." He did, and I forgave her at that point.

"*And comfort*" (v. 7). I was shocked. I knew that word comfort meant encouragement plus alleviation of grief. "But, Lord," I said, "*I'm* the one who's been grieved. I'm supposed to alleviate *her* grief? Lord, You have something turned around."

"No," He said, "you are supposed to comfort, encourage, and alleviate the grief 'lest perhaps such a one should be swallowed up with overmuch sorrow'" (v. 7).

"Lord, do You mean that the person who has grieved me might have a reason for acting that way? Maybe feels threatened? Maybe is struggling?"

I could hear Him say, "Right."

If someone is grieving us, how many of us take the wrong attitude? Though we may not say it in so many words, by our manner we are saying, "I know you're drowning, but I'll just take my foot and push you under to be sure you go down and drown right." Aren't we guilty of this? But God's Word says we are to get underneath, alleviate, and lift! Then, after we do that, we are to:

"*Confirm your love toward him*" (v.8). I began to see that I had no love. Oh, I might have had a little supply of the ordinary love that one has for the members of her church—you know the kind I mean. But it wasn't any special love—there was none of that. In fact, it might have been something just the opposite right then. I'm not sure what I felt, but I know it wasn't deep Christian love.

Then I had to pray, "Lord, give me the love You want me to have for this person." And kneeling by that old pine log, I suddenly had a tremendous sense of God's love being poured upon me. There it was—and I loved her.

But there was a new problem—how to "confirm it." I couldn't get myself to write a letter, but when I reached home I was still convinced that I had to confirm my love to her.

The woman who had grieved me attended the same church I did. (Chris is now Assistant Vice President of Bethel College and is not in the pastorate, so we were attending as members, not as pastor and wife.) On the first Sunday morning we were back in church, I spied her sitting on the opposite side of the sanctuary from me. I didn't hear one word the pastor said as I kept praying, "Lord, if You want me to confirm this love, You have to put her right where I'm going to run into her. I'm not going to make a fool of myself and run over to her."

You know how that kind of prayer goes. Maybe I didn't get quite that hard-nosed, but that's what I was saying to God, "I'm not going to make a fool of myself. You're going to have to put her in my path." And so help me! At the close of the service I opened the big double doors at the back of the sanctuary and almost knocked her down! There she was!

And what did I have to do? I put my arms around her and said only one thing, " I just want you to know I love you." And the tears started to roll.

She said, "And I just want you to know that my husband and I are praying for your Bible study."

She "knew" and I "knew." We got together and really worked it out a few days later.

"That I might know the proof of you" (v.9). Why did I have to go to her? "That I might know the proof of you"—you the member of the prayer group, who is responsible to forgive and to go and confirm his or her love so that God will know how obedient you are—not the one who did the grieving, but the innocent one who was grieved.

"Lest Satan should get an advantage of us" (v. 11). This is the most frightening thing of all. There is nothing the enemy would rather do than to see our prayer groups broken up by our failure to forgive and confirm love. Let's never be guilty of allowing him to "get his foot in the door," for we are not ignorant of his devices.

THIS IS FOR EVERYBODY

I had taught a Sunday School class on this subject of forgiveness, and following the morning service that day, a leading layman who had been in the class said to me, "I just want you to know that two men in our church got together after Sunday School and resolved something that had been between them for many years, and should have been handled long ago."

A man who attended one of our seminars had loaned a relative $70, even though he could hardly spare the money. He shared his feelings with me after our session on forgiving others. "Evelyn," he said, "I just told God that I now forgive the one who borrowed that money a couple of years ago and has not even mentioned it to me since. I was becoming more and more bitter in my heart, and I now know that I have to go and confirm my love to that relative. So, after I get home tonight, I'm going to dig out that little promissory note for the $70 and write on it 'Paid in full,' and put it right in the mail."

For you to do:

1. *Ask God to bring to your mind that person who has grieved you and whom you have not forgiven.*
2. *Ask God to forgive you for the sin of not forgiving that person.*
3. *Now forgive that person, asking God to give you the strength and ability if you need to.*
4. *Now ask God for as much love as He wants you to have for the person who grieved you.*
5. *Next ask God how you should confirm your love to that person.*
6. *Wait in silence for His answer.*
7. *Pray, promising God that you will do whatever He has told you.*
8. *Go do it!*

Praying in One Accord

These all continued with one accord in prayer and supplication, with the women, and Mary the mother of Jesus, and with His brethren. Acts 1:14

v, this is a completely different church from what it was when we left. Why?"

To the returned missionary I replied, "The answer is simple. We have learned to pray in the four years that you and your husband have been in Ethiopia." Then I went on and shared with her how it all started in 1968, the experimentation with prayer techniques, and the method we finally came up with in those days—the small group method of prayer which we call "Praying in One Accord." We found this in God's word, in the Book of Acts:

> And when He had spoken these things, while they beheld, He was taken up; and a cloud received Him out of their sight . . . . Then returned they unto Jerusalem from the mount called Olivet, which is from Jerusalem a Sabbath day's journey. And when they were come in, they went up into an upper room, where abode both Peter, and James, and John, and Andrew, Philip, and Thomas, Bartholomew, and Matthew, James the son of Alpheus, and Simon Zelotes, and Judas the brother of James. *These all continued with one accord in prayer and supplication,* with the

women, and Mary the mother of Jesus and with His brethren (Acts 1:9, 12-14, italics added).

It was a new and exciting experience for us to discover that women were included at this significant time, in the life of the early church. Among them was Mary, the mother of Jesus. In this final reference to her in the New Testament, she's on her face before God, praying with the disciples, the brethren, and the other women. Wouldn't you like to have been with them in the Upper Room? What do you suppose they were praying about? We can't answer that question, but we do know that their hearts were throbbing together as they were praying in one accord.

Jesus, their Lord, had just left Planet Earth. He had gone from their sight, yet the 120 gathered in the Upper Room had the privilege of sensing His presence in their midst. Only a short while before, He had told His disciples, "For where two or three are gathered together in My name, there am I in the midst of them" (Matthew 18:20). Jesus was speaking of those who gather together *in His name*, not of just any group of people who meet together on earth. It is only to His followers that He gives the promise of His presence. Small group praying, the method of praying in one accord, is based on the eligibility to pray in the name of Jesus and pertains only to the followers of Christ.

LORD, TEACH US TO PRAY
We can learn something else from the Upper

Room pray-ers. They were putting into practice what Jesus had taught them about prayer when He was on earth. His disciples must have felt a tremendous lack in their own lives as they saw the beautiful example of the prayer life of their Lord. In their need they cried, "Lord, teach us to pray" (Luke 11:1).

Today earnest followers of the Lord sense their need just as the disciples did. It's amazing that we can knock on doors, get on the telephone, invite people to our prayer groups, only to find that when we meet together we do not know how to pray. I was one of eleven people who formed 5,000 prayer groups for a Billy Graham Crusade held in our area. Afterward we heard that fantastic things had happened in some of those prayer groups where women had prayed for five consecutive weeks before and during the crusade. But hundreds of women said to me "We did everything you told us to do. We knocked on doors, we called our neighbors. We did all these things but we didn't know what to do when we got together. We didn't know how to pray."

Jesus' response to His disciples and to us is simple, yet so beautiful: "When you pray, say, 'Our Father who art in heaven . . . .' " You recognize that, don't you? It's the beginning of what we sometimes call "The Lord's Prayer." What is prayer? *Real prayer is simply conversation with God our Father*. Jesus didn't say, "Now, when you pray, say, 'My Father.'" No, He used the plural, "Our Father." He is your Father, my father, Jesus' Father—"Our Father who art in heaven." It's so simple. Just conversation with God.

CHANGES

When people start praying together in one accord to our Father in heaven, in the name of Jesus, and practice praying together, things begin to change. Our lives change, our families change, our churches change, our communities change. Changes take place not when we study about prayer, not when we talk about it, not even when we memorize beautiful Scripture verses on paper; it is when *we actually pray* that things begin to happen. And we don't suffer from the "paralysis of analysis." We are not paralyzed by analyzing prayer, but we take the problems at hand and pray about them.

A newspaper reporter recently asked me in an interview, "Would you mind telling me how much you charge for these prayer seminars?"

I replied, "We don't charge anything."

"Well, why do you do it? If you don't charge, what is your reason for spending all this time and effort?"

I had to stop and think a minute. Then I said, "The reason I teach people to pray is that I have seen so many changed lives as a result of prayer. This is what makes it so exciting. We learn not *about* prayer, but *to pray*, to converse with our Father who is in heaven."

One day I received an invitation from the women of another church to come over and teach them to pray. I said I would. A few days later, as we drove along the main street in her little red Volkswagen, the woman who picked me up took her eyes off the road and looking straight at me asked, "Do you care if our pastor comes this afternoon?"

I was quiet for a minute because I have a "thing" about this. I thought, "Who am I to be teaching pastors?"

She assured me, "He really wants to come."

I said, "Okay, if he really wants to come, you tell him it's all right." So the pastor sat way back in one corner of the room while the women of his church, many of whom had never prayed out loud before, learned our six little S's of prayer. Afterward we broke into smaller groups, and I know that 100 percent of those women prayed that day.

A week later at a Sunday School dinner meeting, I was sitting one place away from the speaker, who was the assistant pastor of that same church. During the meal he leaned over and loudly announced to me, "Say, do you know you turned our church upside down?"

I asked, "What happened?"

He replied, "Well, ever since our pastor heard the women praying, and learned how all this prayer works, he won't let us have single meeting unless we pray. We can't even have a book review in our church unless we pray about it!" He didn't seem too happy about it.

"I didn't turn your church upside down," I replied. "But it's very possible that God did."

Recently a pastor greeted me at the door when I arrived to speak to the women of his church. "I'm so glad finally to see what you look like. A woman is here today who attended the prayer seminar in downtown Minneapolis. She bought a set of your tapes, and has been a little missionary circulating them among the women's circles for the last eleven months. Each circle has had its own mini-prayer seminar, with the women learning to pray. I can see such a difference in their lives."

NOT FOR WOMEN ONLY

One night in the fall of 1969 my husband bounced in from a deacon board meeting with a message for me: "Will you please ask the women if they will take our annual Prayer Week the first week in January."

Right away I shot back the answer. I didn't stop to pray. I didn't ask God what He thought about it. I just said to Chris, "You tell your deacon board no. God has called me to teach women." But I wasn't really being honest with God.

My husband trotted back to the board and told them, "There's no way they're going to teach the whole church how to pray."

The board said, "You go back to your wife and tell her that we have been watching and we feel that the women have discovered a method of prayer that works, and we would like them to teach it to the whole church."

By this time my husband was becoming like a Ping-Pong ball being batted back and forth between two paddles—the deacon board and me. When Chris returned with the same request, I realized that I had been hasty in my reply the first time.

I said, "All right, I'll take it to the women."

Their response was also negative.

At this point I suggested that we pray about it. After fervent prayer we concluded that the deacons' request was really God's way of speaking to us. We consented to take Prayer Week for 1970 on one condition—that it be held the second week in January, the first being preparation week. The board agreed. That first week we trained prayer group leaders representing every department of the church—the choir, the deacon board, the trustee board, and the Sunday School. They all came to learn the ground rules for effective praying.

In the week of prayer that followed, we discovered that we had about five times as many people participating as we ever had in the past. There were boys and girls, men and women—preschoolers to golden agers—from every area of our church life, all learning to *pray in one accord*. I don't know of one person who didn't pray, but I'll stay on the side of caution and say that of all those who attended, 95 percent actively participated in audible prayer. Now, that's a lot of people praying, and there were some very definite answers that gave us great encouragement.

I recall how thrilled the members of the Junior Department were after I had taught them our method of praying in one accord on the Sunday morning during Prayer Week. They came up with two urgent needs: "We need a superintendent and a piano player in our department." That morning the juniors with their teachers divided into small groups and prayed specifically that God would send them these workers. I cringed a little inside. What if God didn't answer their prayer?

On the following Wednesday, one of the church's businessmen came to Gail, our children's worker, and said, "The Lord has laid it on my heart to be superintendent of the Junior Department, and my wife would like to play the piano for the juniors, if she can be replaced in her present department."

Meanwhile God had been working in the college class also. On the same Sunday, along with specific prayer, they were offering themselves to God for service in the church. A student nurse wrote on her card, "I am available to play the piano where I'm needed." Gail assigned the student nurse to replace the wife in the other department, and the following Sunday the juniors almost exploded with excitement as they were presented their new superintendent and pianist. God had really answered their prayers!

IN ONE ACCORD

We, as women of the church, had simply shared the method that God had given to us from the Bible, the method of praying in one accord in small groups. How is this achieved? *Simply by praying about only one subject at a time with one person praying aloud while the others in the group are praying silently on the same subject.* In this way everyone is praying together, in one accord, instead of planning other prayers in advance.

Have you ever been in a group when someone is praying a long prayer? And have you found that you were not really praying along with that person? Instead, you were mulling over in your mind all the things you were going to pray about when your turn came? I have, and my thoughts have run like this, "Lord, now bring to my mind. . . . Oh, I don't want to forget that one. . . . Say, that's a good request. . . . Thank You, Lord, for reminding me of that one." Then I have gone back and reviewed the prayer subjects on my fingers. Next, I've wondered what my introductory statement should be, or how I should conclude my prayer. While someone else has been praying, I have been planning my own long prayer in advance, instead of praying silently on the same subject with the person who is praying audibly. That's not praying in one accord.

You see, if everyone in a group is praying in one accord with the person who is praying aloud, the total number of prayers ascending to heaven is multiplied by the number who are praying silently. How much more power there is in prayer when all the participants are praying in one accord!

For you to pray:

Father, teach me to pray in one accord with other people, sharing their burdens, joys, and petitions.

The Method—Six S's

But when ye pray, use not vain repetitions, as the heathen do; for they think that they shall be heard for their much speaking. Be not ye therefore like unto them, for your Father knoweth what things ye have need of, before ye ask Him. Matthew 6:7-8

ell, I suppose you all know how to pray. I won't fit into this group." With that remark, Betty, my neighbor, joined the three of us meeting in a home on our block to pray for the coming Billy Graham Crusade. There she was, apparently wanting to take part, but scared to death to pray aloud, even with only three other women present.

There are thousands of people just like Betty. They are all over the country—in neighborhood prayer groups, in midweek services, and in special prayer sessions—and they are not praying audibly for only one reason: *they don't know how.*

We have found in our prayer seminars that about 50 percent of those participating have never prayed aloud before. They come from a great variety of churches, Protestant and Catholic, but talking with God in the presence of others is a very real problem to them.

My response to my neighbor, Betty, was, "Oh, yes, you certainly will fit into this group. It's really not difficult. After we hear the prayer requests, we all are going to pray just one simple sentence on each one." And we did. The three of us, who had prayed for years, prayed one simple sentence following the request, and so did Betty! In fact, as we concluded that session, she had prayed four times audibly. What happens when we put ourselves on the level of the most inexperienced pray-ers? Many of them hear their own voices in prayer for the first time.

The rules we applied that morning were the ones our women devised in 1968 to implement our method of praying in one accord—praying about only one subject at a time, with one person praying aloud while the others in the group are praying silently on the same subject. There are Six S's, six simple rules to follow, whether one is a participant or a prayer group leader, a seasoned pray-er or a shy and untrained one. These six rules serve as effective tools to help a prayer group get started, to encourage newcomers, and to motivate timid people to pray aloud. But a prayer group doesn't have to stay with these elementary rules. It's exciting to know that the participants can go on and graduate into effective, fervent, spontaneous praying.

Suppose your present prayer group is not going very well, with no one wanting to join or perhaps not coming back after trying it once. Or, suppose you would like to start a prayer group in your church or in your neighborhood. You may find that these Six S's are just what you need to encourage 100 percent participation.

1. SUBJECT BY SUBJECT

The first "S" is *Subject by Subject*—praying in one

accord about only one subject at a time. As one person prays out loud, the rest pray silently on the same subject, *not planning their own prayers in advance*. This assures complete concentration and fervent prayer on one request at a time. Also, in this way no one is deprived of the privilege of praying for the request before going on to another.

You may be accustomed to praying around the world, mentioning every person you know, every missionary in many different countries. And, as a prayer group leader, you may be tempted to pray this way. But your part is only to announce one subject for prayer at a time, and then to pray a short sentence prayer yourself. Sometimes it's a good idea to have a list ready and to say, "Right now we are going to pray one simple sentence about _____." Then, as the leader, pray one simple sentence and wait for others to pray audibly on the same subject before going to the next request. Because the participants will have to "shift mental gears" before going on to another subject, it's a good idea to pause between subjects. Then the group will be prepared to pray again.

As the participants learn to pray in one accord, subject by subject, prayer gains momentum and becomes more spontaneous. When this happens, the leader may simply lead out in prayer on a subject rather than announcing it. When those in our groups become proficient in this method, their spiritual pulses will be throbbing together in such a way that each one will begin to sense the direction of the Holy Spirit when it is time to start a new subject. Everyone in the group will then have the freedom to initiate a new topic for prayer. It may take a while, but this is our goal. They don't have to have a leader anymore!

I remember the first time I tried this with my group, in 1968. I had always come to the prayer meeting with a written list of requests at which I would peek with one eye. That day I told God I was going to hide the list and trust Him completely to bring to the minds of the pray-ers those things He wanted us to remember in prayer. Checking the list after we finished praying, I was delighted and amazed to find that He had reminded someone to pray about every single request I had written down!

When praying subject by subject, everyone is free to pray audibly in turn. But whether praying audibly or silently, all are praying in one accord on the same subject, not planning their own prayers in advance, but multiplying the power of all the prayers that are ascending simultaneously to God's throne.

2. SHORT PRAYERS
Short Prayers, the second handle, are the secret of the success of small group prayer. Just one, or only a few sentences from each person on each subject allows time for all to pray if they wish. No one should be forced to pray aloud; let prayer be spontaneous, something a person wants to do, even if it's only to hear her own voice in prayer.

As leaders we are responsible to see that the prayers are short. How are we going to do this? Superimpose our wills on our groups and say, "Look everybody, let's pray short prayers"? No, but at first *we* will have to back way up and start praying just one simple sentence ourselves in order to get the shy, untrained ones to pray. We can make the rest of the group more comfortable by the kind of praying we do. Might it be that God is much more interested in the short statement of a new pray-er who has never prayed audibly before, than He is in an elaborate prayer uttered by one who has had years of practice? It may be that we, veteran pray-ers, mature pray-ers, are inhibiting the shy ones. Some of us might even have the idea that God hears us for our "much praying."

Christ had something to say about this when He was teaching His disciples to pray!

> But when ye pray, use not vain repetitions, as the heathen do; for they think that they shall be heard for their much speaking. Be not ye therefore like unto them, for your Father knoweth what things ye have need of, before ye ask Him (Matthew 6:7-8).

Do we think we're going to be heard because we give an introduction, three points, and a conclusion to everything we pray about? God knows all we need, and all we have to do is to lay our requests before Him. Just think of all the requests that go unremembered when someone dominates the group with lengthy prayers on one, two, or even three subjects!

There are, of course, times when long, involved prayers are very much in order. If you are asked to lead in prayer at a meeting and respond by praying one simple sentence, you will probably jar the whole group! Long prayers are appropriate at the right time and place, but that time is not when the shy and untrained are learning to pray.

3. SIMPLE PRAYERS

The third "S" is *Simple Prayers*. Those who have never prayed before will find it possible to utter one *simple* sentence from the heart when the leaders and other participants avoid using complicated phrases and a special prayer vocabulary. When we leave our high-sounding theological expressions at home in our prayer closets and make our short prayers simple ones, then the new pray-ers will feel comfortable about praying one simple, uncomplicated prayer themselves, and will be more apt to return the following week.

Though he didn't know it at the time, I learned a valuable lesson from one of our church leaders during our Prayer Week in 1970. He was an Irishman with a beautiful accent and a rich vocabulary. Whenever he prayed aloud, our hearts soared heavenward. But we had a problem. When he finished praying nobody else dared to follow him! Why, I wouldn't be caught dead praying after he had just uttered his long, beautiful prayer, couched in lofty theological phrases. I can remember even my husband hesitating to close in prayer after this man had prayed so eloquently.

As we approached that 1970 Prayer Week, I wondered what was going to happen in a group he would be leading. I soon found out, for one night he and I were leading our respective groups in areas separated only by a plastic curtain. As I presented the prayer requests to my group, I found it difficult to concentrate because I was so curious to learn what was happening on the other side of the curtain. Have you ever had your ear attuned in one direction while your voice was aimed in another?

I heard him open his prayer group with just one simple sentence. Astounded, I listened for more, but he didn't say another word. Soon, one by one, all the people in his group prayed their own simple sentences. Then he prayed another sentence on the next subject and stopped. Once again each one prayed. I was acquainted with everyone in his group, and I knew that many of them had never prayed aloud before; but that night every single person in his circle prayed aloud. What happens when we are willing to put ourselves temporarily on the level of those who don't know how to pray? We encourage them to pray with us.

Back in 1968 when we were practicing and experimenting with all these methods, eventually a whole room in our church was filled with women praying; but Eva, a woman who lived next door to the church, declared that she would not join the others in prayer. She said she had never prayed out loud in a group and never would.

I knew that Eva's family had a very fine devotional life. She was a great Christian. That wasn't her problem, but praying aloud with others was. She would shake her finger at me in other meetings and say, "Don't you ever call on me to pray; don't you ever call on me!"

I assured her that we never call on anybody to pray, but still she didn't come to our prayer meetings. As we drove up to the church, we would see the curtains part as she peeked out the window, but that's as close as Eva got. Then one day, without explanation, she joined us. She came every week after that, but never prayed out loud.

As the summer rolled around, we moved our meetings to one the parks in town. It was at one of those park sessions that I had a distinct impression from God that Eva was going to pray that day. But as I led the group in prayer, mentioning one request after another, she didn't utter a word. Though it was past time for us to start home, I kept adding requests and waiting for her. Suddenly, Eva began to pray. She forgot all the rules she ever learned. It was like Niagara Falls breaking loose! That day Eva prayed around the world.

When we had Prayer Week in January 1970, one of the groups praying was made up of all men, including the pastor and the chairman of the church board, except Eva. Again my ear was attuned in another direction. Guess who prayed *first* in that group? Eva! She has said to me since, "Ev, if I can do it, *anybody* can."

4. SPECIFIC PRAYER REQUESTS

Handle number four is *Specific Prayer Requests*. Specific requests listed and specific answers noted are a great encouragement to continuing and expanded prayer. Use a notebook to list your requests and answers.

If groups start falling apart, and they may, or if people suddenly aren't interested, the best way to get things going again is to encourage them by showing specific answers to their specific requests. When there's a lag, whip out that little book in which requests and answers are recorded and point out how God had used the prayer group to change circumstances and individuals. Spend time in prayer *praising God* for His specific answers. Then watch as new life floods your prayer group!

As the specific answers to their prayers pile up, you will begin to see the pray-ers change as well. By keeping records, the individuals who are praying start to *see the worth of themselves in prayer*, and this is important.

Date your specific requests and date the answers. God is not controlled by time as we human beings are. He places His answers down on Planet Earth when He knows it is best. Therefore, if we keep track of *time*—how long God takes to answer our prayers—we're going to learn some tremendous spiritual lessons about how God operates. As weeks and months and years come and go, we will see that His timing is always perfect.

We will also learn some *whys* when we keep track of how He answers. It may be that we are not ready for some answers. My two prayer partners and I prayed every week for two solid years before I had my first neighborhood Bible study. I wasn't ready and God knew I wasn't. If we keep a record of the specific timing of our requests and God's answers, then we can look back and see many of the reasons for His delays and His withholdings.

God may answer our prayers not only at a time when we least expect, but He may answer in a *way* we don't expect. We will be astounded at how God answers prayer. He may answer in a way that is completely opposite to the way we think He should. He knows what is best for us, and He never makes a mistake.

Our women experienced this great joy in praying specifically in May 1968, when we were preparing for a mother-daughter banquet. Ruth Johnson of "Back to the Bible Broadcast," and a daughter of our church, was to be the speaker. We set up a prayer room and asked the women who came to the church to work (cook, set tables, decorate) to spend some time, equal time if they could, in the prayer room praying specifically for Ruth Johnson. What a great moving of God there was at the banquet that night!

On the following Sunday, with my little notebook in hand (I always recorded the results of our prayer experimentation), I said to Ruth, "Please be very careful how you answer me because we zeroed in on you in prayer, and I want a very honest answer. This will be reported to our national conference in June. Will you tell me what happened, if anything did happen, on Friday night when you spoke at our banquet?"

Ruth drew a deep breath and tears came to her eyes. "Ev," she said, "the last time I was in this church it was to bury my mother. It all came back to me last Friday as I was on my way here. After I got to the church, I couldn't even bring myself to open the door. I kept thinking of my mother, and then I thought of my former Sunday School teachers who were going to be at the banquet. You know, I used to be 'naughty little Ruthie' to those teachers, and I had a feeling that they were all going to be looking at me and thinking, *There's that 'naughty little Ruthie' again.* Evelyn, I could not walk through that door. But suddenly, I felt a great sense of strength and freedom. I can't explain it, but there was complete release and I walked in. It was just fantastic. My voice has gone around the world via radio for thirty years, but never in all those years have I felt such freedom and such power as I experienced when I sang and spoke last Friday night."

Not long afterward Ruth's missionary brother came home from India. He came to me and said, "Evie, what did you do to my sister?"

I replied, "We didn't do anything to your sister."

He said, "Oh, yes you did. Since the women prayed, my sister has been a completely different woman."

Now I thought Ruth was a fantastic Christian before that time, but I learned something. It was that we don't limit our praying to the down-and-outer, or to someone we think is dying or experiencing great tragedy. We also need to pray for those who are ministering, who don't appear to have any needs. What did we do? We only prayed—specifically. And God worked.

5. SILENT PERIODS

The fifth "S" is *Silent Periods.* Silent periods between prayers are a privilege and a blessing. Don't panic when there's a lull—just listen! Prayer is *a two-way conversation* with God.

Today silence is almost a lost art. After a few seconds pass without audible prayer, someone usually feels compelled to clear her throat, shuffle her feet, or nervously finger a songbook. Somehow we think we have to talk at God all of the time, but there are marvelous things God wants to say to us. He has answers to our questions, secrets He wants to share, and yet we bombard Him with our "much praying." We forget that God is on His throne in heaven just waiting to say something great to us, if we would only give Him a chance. How frustrated He must be (if God can become frustrated) when He has something so wonderful to tell you and me, and we aren't quiet long enough to listen to what He has to say.

One day when I asked my son about a girl who lives near us, he said, "Oh, I guess she's fine, Mom, if she'd ever keep still so we could find out."

"What do you mean?" I asked.

"Well, on the school bus that girl talks every single minute. She might be a real great girl, but she doesn't shut up long enough for us to find out."

Has God ever thought that about me? About you? Have we learned to keep still long enough for God to say something to us? It is in the *silence* that our communication becomes two-way.

The first time I practiced the Six-S method at a retreat was in 1969. It was evening, and as the women finished praying in their small groups of four, I dismissed them to go out to a point near the water. "Just one rule," I said. "Please don't talk while you are walking out to the point." There had been fervent prayer in their groups, and I wanted them to keep their hearts open to God's voice.

We had planned that the KTIS radio trio would come to the point by boat and, at a given signal, sing to the women on shore. But the signal somehow failed, and they waited and waited, not knowing when to start their song. The leader of the testimony meeting kept putting more wood on the fire and thinking, "I *have* to say something." But each time she thought it, God said, "Keep still, Mary." In fact, Mary told me later, "You know very well, Evelyn, that God said, 'Mary, shut up!' "

Twenty minutes went by with about 500 women sitting in absolute silence at the water's edge. Now and then we could hear soft crying. Then from the boat totally obscured by the darkness, came the beautiful strains of "Take my life and let it be, consecrated Lord to Thee." The common theme that ran through the testimonies that night was: "God spoke to me not so much in the songs or in the message, but in the silence."

6. SMALL GROUPS

Small Groups, the sixth "S," are usually best for newcomers, as well as for the shy or untrained. For some, it would take great courage to stand before hundreds of people and raise their voices in prayer for the first time. But in smaller groups they can gain confidence in praying audibly.

In our seminars when there are several hundred participants in one room, we divide into small groups of four or five. This is quickly accomplished by standing and having every other row turn back, each two rows of people facing each other. We then just draw apart in groups of four, two from each row. How my heart thrilled at one of our prayer seminars in a large church when almost 200 small groups of people in the same room lifted their voices earnestly to God.

Yesterday, when one of my original prayer partners called me long distance, we chatted about the joy and the privilege of being just two or three in a little group. "Ev," she recalled, "when we started praying, just the three of us, that was the turning point in my spiritual life."

Whatever we do, we must never underestimate the value of a small group praying, for Christ promised that *where two or three of His followers are gathered together in His name, He will be in their midst* (see Matthew 18:20). What an opportunity it provides to practice the presence of Christ in our midst!

Do you remember in the account of the stoning of Stephen that he lifted up his eyes and "saw the glory of God, and Jesus standing on the right hand of God"? (Acts 7:55) The right hand of God is the place of authority and honor. Christ is still at the right hand of God today, interceding for us, but we also have His promise that He will be with us—where even two or three are gathered together.

Now, we want to be very careful that we do not take Christ off His throne, that we do not play games with Him in prayer. He is in heaven, but His presence is in the midst of those who gather together in His name.

Christ helped the disciples and those who know Him very intimately here on earth to understand this. G. Campbell Morgan, in his message "Rekindled Fire," emphasizes the importance of our Lord's vanishing and appearing after His resurrection. He explains that the disciples and His friends were learning the lesson that Christ was with them, even when they did not see Him with their physical eyes. These followers of Jesus were practicing His presence even though they could not see Him. After He had vanished from their sight for the last time at His ascension, He was in their midst in the Upper Room, and they knew it.

For you to pray:

Dear Father, Please give me the privilege of being aware of the presence of Jesus, my Savior, in a prayer group. Teach me to help others to pray. Teach me to listen to You speaking to me in the silent periods.

How to Pray in God's Will

*And this is the confidence that we have in Him,
that, if we ask anything according to His will, He
heareth us. And if we know that He hear us, whatsoever we ask, we know that we have the petitions
that we desired of Him.* 1 John 5:14-15

On the morning following the funeral of Lindon Karo, a St. Paul pastor, I posed some searching questions to those attending our prayer seminar. "What do you think went wrong? Why did this tremendous pastor, only thirty-two years old, die of cancer? Thousands of prayers were offered for him. Forty people in his church had covenanted to fast and pray one day a week for him. I don't think I attended a meeting anywhere during that period, but that we were all praying. Why weren't those prayers answered? What went wrong? Why did we bury Lindon Karo yesterday?"

When I reached this point in the seminar, a steering committee member wanting to be helpful waved her hand from the back of the church, and said, "Yes, Evelyn, and Lindon Karo's mother-in-law and sister-in-law are here."

Wow! I stopped for a second and pondered, "Do I go on? Do I insult these people by teaching a lesson on how to pray in God's will? What do I do about these loved ones who buried their son-in-law and brother-in-law just yesterday?" What would you have done? I felt God was telling me to go ahead and teach the lesson.

When the session was over, those two very beautiful Christian women came to me and said, "Please don't worry about today's lesson. Many months ago we as a family committed the whole matter of Lindon's illness to the Lord. We prayed, 'Only Your will, God, whatever it is.' We did not ask for healing only; we prayed that God's will be done in our loved one's life."

Have you come to the place where you can pray, "Only God's will"? Do you know that you are in absolute oneness with the will of God? Have you come to that place?

We read in 1 John 5:14-15 about a prerequisite to effective praying. "And this is the confidence that we have in Him, that if we ask anything according to His will, He heareth us. And if we know that He hear us, whatsoever we ask, we know that we have the petitions that we desired of Him." Did you catch the prerequisite? How can we have confidence in anything we ask? By praying *according to His will*. And what is confidence in prayer? It is knowing absolutely and irrevocably that we have whatever we have asked.

"IF IT BE THY WILL, AMEN"

What do we mean when we use the expression "praying in God's will"? Is it simply tacking on the end of a prayer the phrase we use perhaps more frequently than any other? You know how it goes. We ask God for a whole string of things, then we piously add, "If it be Thy will, Lord. Amen." Or, it may be that we even ask God for something we know is not good for us. Let's say, for example, that we ask for a bushel of Hershey bars! God knows very well (and so do we) that if we ate a bushel of Hershey bars we'd die of indigestion; but many times we ask Him for something just as ridiculous and tack on, "If it be Thy will," just to get ourselves off the hook. This is not what it means to pray in God's will.

THE PRAYING PERSON—
NOT THE PRAYER REQUEST

Berkeley Mickelsen, formerly professor of New Testament Greek at Bethel Seminary, said to me one day, "Evelyn, I hope that when you're teaching all those women to pray in God's will that you are teaching them that it is the person praying, and not the prayer request, that changes."

I said, "Berkeley, that's the whole gist of our lesson on God's will."

Praying in God's will is not easy, yet it's very simple. It involves a commitment of every single thing that comes into our lives to God and His perfect will. And it's exciting to live in complete oneness with the will of God. It is never dull or static because it is not a one-time, once-for-all commitment. It is something we have to work at constantly, moment by moment.

This is expressed in a beautiful definition of the word *effectual* as it is found in James 5:16. According to *Vine's Expository Dictionary of New Testament Words*, it means "the effect produced in the praying person, bringing him into line with the will of God." It is the pray-er who changes rather than the prayer. Praying "in the will of God" means *being* conformed to the will of God as we pray. Wouldn't it be great if we could *always be conformed to the will of God*, with all known sin confessed, so that we would never pray outside the will of God? The effectual pray-er, then, is a person who is completely committed to God's will for answers, and not to his own will.

After our women had been praying for a few months back in 1968, my husband exclaimed one day, "Wow, if God doesn't answer a single one of your prayers, what He's doing *in* the people who are praying will be worth it all."

What God does in the lives of people who are praying, in bringing them in line with His will, is one of His miracles here on Planet Earth. The turning point in our Prayer Seminars is the session where people in prayer commit their whole lives to God's perfect will. This happened to a college teacher who sent me this note:

> On February 26 my sister invited me to attend your prayer seminar. I thought, *A prayer seminar? What good will it do? I have prayed and prayed, and it hasn't done any good.* But I went.
>
> You see, I have been a Christian all of my life. I was raised in a wonderful Christian home and reared in an atmosphere of loving and trusting Jesus. But, suddenly, I was faced with very severe testing of my faith. My hus-

band's construction company folded, leaving a large sum of debts for which we were 50 percent responsible.

Because of this, we had to sell our home and liquidate our assets.

Also, I was not well, and our little two-year-old son had just undergone surgery.

Then, the Scripture that was to change my life and my prayers, 1 John 5:14-15, "And this is the confidence. . . ." Up to that point I had not prayed for His will. I could only see what I wanted to happen.

Evelyn, you asked us to stand at the end of the session and form our prayer groups of four. You told us to ask God for the *one* thing we wanted most from Him. I remember saying aloud in my little circle of four Christian sisters, "Lord, I want Your perfect will for me and my family."

That was it! I was to learn later that was what was keeping my prayers from being answered. I had never asked God for His will.

Now, I felt entirely free. I felt the whole load lift, as if the responsibility to straighten up the messy things was not mine. Now it is nine months since that time, and I cannot begin to tell you the peace I have in my heart. My husband's business debts are not all cleared up as yet, but God is moving. The burden is lifted. My health has improved tremendously. In fact, I got a teaching position at Bethel College this fall, a position that just seemed to come right out of heaven itself. I was not applying or seeking such a position, but was asked to join the staff. Praise God! He can "do exceeding abundantly above all that we ask or think" (Ephesians 3:20).

ON EARTH, AS IT IS IN HEAVEN

For us to pray, "Lord, I want Your will down here on earth," is a tremendous prayer. Wouldn't it be fantastic if we could pray that for Washington, D.C. today? If we would by our praying get God's will done in Moscow, or in the Middle East? While there is a sense in which we can pray that God's will be done in these places, they are not within our direct sphere of influence, are they? But there is a spot on earth that belongs only to you. It is your own personal sphere. It has been given to you by our Heavenly Father. And it's possible for you to bring about God's complete will in your sphere of influence here on earth.

The disciples whom Jesus taught to pray: "Our Father . . . Thy will be done on earth as it is in heaven," knew they couldn't change the whole Roman Empire, but they also knew it was possible for them to change the spheres of influence which had been given to them by God. And they did. God frequently changes circumstances and people when we in a very personal way pray that His will be done in our own spheres of influence.

The Lord's Prayer really comes into focus right

where we are when we pray, "Thy will be done on earth as it is in heaven." Is there anything contrary to God's will in heaven? No! Think of what would happen if every Christian really brought God's will to the little sphere that is his or hers, with nothing contrary to God's perfect will! How different would be our nation, our cities, our churches, our homes.

THE EXAMPLE OF CHRIST

The supreme example of praying in the will of God is that of Christ praying in the Garden of Gethsemane on the night before He was to die on the cross for our sins. Our Lord, in His humanity, did not want to suffer. He prayed, "Father, if Thou be willing, remove this cup from Me; nevertheless not My will, but Thine, be done" (Luke 22:42). Then, after much agony of spirit, He said, "Father, I am willing for Your will."

Have you come to the place in your life where you can say, "Lord, not my will, but Thine be done. No matter how much it hurts, how difficult the task, how high the mountain You've given me to climb, it doesn't make any difference, dear Lord, I am willing"?

When we visited the Holy Land a few years ago, I sat alone under one of those old, gnarled olive trees in the Garden of Gethsemane and read in Luke's Gospel the account of all my Jesus went through the night before He died, before He took upon Himself the sin of the world, including mine; when He sweat as it were great drops of blood there in the garden. With my heart absolutely breaking, I wrote in the margin of my Bible, "Lord, please, only Your will in my life, only Your will!" We don't have to sit under an ancient olive tree in His land to come to that place, but right where we are today we can say to Christ, "Lord, not my will, only Yours be done."

When we reach the place where we're really on our faces before God, does He as an "ogre" sitting up in heaven say, "Good, I have another doormat on which to wipe My feet"? Is that what He says? Do we become doormats for God to wipe His feet on when we say, "Lord, I'm willing for Your will"? Oh, no. What happened to Christ the day after He said this to His Heavenly Father? He became the *Redeemer of mankind*! He became your Savior and my Savior.

Mary too had a tremendous privilege because she was willing for God's will in her life. Do you recall her response at the time of the Annunciation? When the angel came to her and said that God had chosen her to be the mother of the Savior, Mary immediately responded, "Behold, the handmaid of the Lord; be it according to Thy word."

Do you think it was easy for Mary to say yes to the will of God, to being pregnant out of wedlock? When it meant vulnerability to misunderstanding, to ridicule? When it could mean possible rejection by her fiancé or even being stoned to death? It was not easy for Mary, but because she was willing for God's will, she was greatly blessed by Him. She was given the great privilege of bearing the Son who became our Redeemer.

OPEN DOORS
What happens to me when I am on my face

before God and say, "Okay, Lord, I don't know what You want. That's a big mountain, that's difficult surgery, these are hard things in my life; but, Lord, no matter what it is, I want Your perfect will"? At that point does God become an ogre and take advantage of my commitment? No, at that point He starts to open doors, and fantastic things begin to happen— even prayer seminars—when I just make myself available to Him.

One day our campus pastor inquired, "Ev, how did you ever get all those prayer seminars started, anyway?"

I shrugged. "They just sort of grew, like Topsy." He looked at me, wondering what I was saying. I went on, "You know, we really didn't plan them. They just happened. In every single step, the constant prayer of steering committees, prayer chains, and our advisory board has been, 'Lord, Your will.' Then we wait to see what His will is. We never even make contacts asking to hold a seminar, and it is so thrilling to watch God work when we let Him."

One day a young woman who had traveled almost 100 miles round trip each day to attend a Minneapolis prayer seminar asked me, " What is the procedure to get you to come to our town for a prayer seminar?"

I replied, "Pray about it, and if it is God's will, we'll come."

"Oh, three of us have been praying for several months," she replied, "and we believe God is saying we should have it."

"That's good enough for me," I said. "I'll come."

I better understood her insistence on having a semi-nar in her town when she handed me this note:

> Dear Evelyn, Since being in your prayer seminar at Elim Lutheran Church, my life has been changed through accepting Christ. Also, my four-year-old daughter and nine-year-old son have asked Jesus into their lives. Now my husband wants me to work on him. Thank You.

God rewarded her eagerness when thirty women found Christ in her seminar. It was God's will!

In fact, the Bible study on prayer for all the churches in White Bear Lake, Minnesota, that auto-matically turned into our first prayer seminar, came into being because God took over. The chairman and I, frustrated at not being able to work my schedule into all the fall events of that area, finally in tears just prayed together, "All right, Lord, only *Your* will. Whenever *You* want this Bible study, work it out." And God timed it perfectly. He knew all along when prayer would be needed in that town. He knew that the next February, witches and occult personnel would be in one of the high schools, so He planned for those 250 women to be "praying in one accord" just at the right time.

This whole prayer ministry started in November 1967, when I was asked to work on the prayer exper-iment that I described in chapter 1. I hesitated at first, not knowing for certain whether to make the com-mitment. But one day, while I was reading God's

Word, a phrase in Revelation, "Behold, I have set before thee an open door," stood out as if it were in bold print. God said, "Evelyn, I have set before *you* an open door." I closed my Bible, said, "Lord, I'm willing," and went to the phone and dialed long distance to Chicago. I said excitedly to the executive secretary of our National Women's Board, "How can I say no when God has just put before me an open door in Revelation 3:8?"

Has God put before you an open door? Are you hesitating, perhaps rebelling, or holding back because of fear, when God is challenging, "Look, here's an open door, wouldn't you like to walk through it for Me? This is My will for you"?

Oh, answer Him, "Lord, here I am. There is no friction between my will and Yours. Whatever You have for me, I know that You will give me enough strength, enough grace. I know You will give me all that I need. Lord, I am ready to do Your will."

"Try it. You'll like it!" It's amazing what happens when we step out.

MEN TOO?

Sometimes I seem to need a little help from other people in going through the doors God is opening for me. "I don't think God is hung up on you teaching men to pray, but I think *you* are," a professional Christian counselor chided as we chatted at a Christmas party. I suddenly realized that I was so hung up that I was praying, "God, Your will," but didn't have the courage to accept it.

My prayer chains had been praying for several

months about frequent requests from men to attend prayer seminars. Then I learned that while I was planning to give a three-minute speech the next Sunday encouraging attendance at our upcoming seminar, the host church was planning for me to present *the* morning message. I was panicking, just *knowing* it never could be God's will for me to do *that*!

Suddenly, as we were together praying, a prayer chain member prayed, "Lord, we're sick and tired of praying this request. We're going to put out a fleece. The way the men accept Evelyn next Sunday morning will be our answer as to whether she opens the prayer seminar to men or not." I nearly fainted as she prayed. *I* never would have dared talk to God like that.

The next Saturday I received a call from a woman in one of St. Paul's suburbs. "I've met with some of our deacons (we're between pastors), and we want an evening prayer seminar in our church that is open to men, women, and young people. We definitely feel it is God's will."

"I'll give you my answer on Monday," I stalled, not daring to tell her I had to see how the "fleece" came out the next day!

With fear and trembling I shared "What Happens When We Pray" with the Sunday congregation. After the service the knuckles on my right hand were white from so many men shaking hands and thanking me. Nine days later we started our first prayer seminar for women *and men*. Sometimes I need a little pushing to go through doors God is opening. Do you?

IF YOU WANT ME, LORD

One Friday afternoon during our first prayer seminar, I asked my small telephone prayer chain of ten members to pray that God would keep my schedule in balance speaking against the occult and on prayer. That night, in one of those deep devotional times that come periodically in many of our lives, I prayed, "Lord, I don't know what it is, but I want Your will, just Your will." And I meant it. Then, out of the blue it seemed—but I'm sure it was God-inspired—I heard myself promising God that I would be involved in two areas if He wanted me to. One was the Billy Graham Crusade which was to be held that coming summer; the other was a national women's prayer movement.

The very next morning my telephone rang. It was Myrl Glockner. She said, "Evelyn, we've never met, but I just felt I had to call and ask if you will be one of the eleven committee members to get 5,000 prayer groups going for the Billy Graham Crusade. Do you want time to pray about it?"

I was stunned. "Myrl," I stammered, "I don't need time to pray. How can I say no when just last night I said so completely, 'Lord, Your will, if You want me to be involved in the Billy Graham Crusade.'"

On the following Tuesday, after I had completed a prayer seminar session, a woman came down the aisle of the church waving a paper and calling, "Evelyn, I have a message here for you from Vonette Bright of the Great Commission Prayer Crusade. She would like you to become involved in the program."

Friday, Saturday, and Tuesday. There it was—God's opening of two doors when I told Him I was willing for His will for me with those two organizations. It's a very exciting thing. Don't say, "I want it my way, Lord," but, "Lord, Your way. Whatever You have for me, I'm Yours. You just take me, open any door, lead me in any direction." You will be astounded at what God will do. You will be panting, trying to keep up with the opportunities. Phone calls will come from people you didn't even know existed. Who inspired that person to call and ask you to go here or there to minister? Nobody—but God.

For you to pray:

O God, I want only Your will in my life. Open the doors You have for me, and give me the courage and faith to go through them.

GOD NEVER MAKES A MISTAKE

Wherefore let them that suffer according to the will of God commit the keeping of their soul to Him in well doing, as unto a faithful Creator. 1 Peter 4:19

 n order to pray effectively in God's will, you may need a new view of God—as One who never makes a mistake. Our daughter Jan was still in high school when a friend of hers was in a serious automobile accident just before Labor Day. Not knowing whether Rick was dead or alive, she went down to the courthouse to see his demolished car, which had been placed on the lawn by city officials to serve as a gruesome reminder to weekend travelers.

I was standing at the kitchen sink doing dishes when Jan came in trembling. Describing the car, she wondered how they ever pried Rick out of that crushed front seat. Suddenly she said, "But, Mom, God never makes a mistake!" And turning on her heels, she flew upstairs sobbing and threw herself across her bed.

It was a few years later while she was in college that Jan came home because our family was going through a crisis. Once again she stepped into that same kitchen, and after we had wept together, she backed off, raised her finger at me and said, "Now, Mom, don't *you* forget, God makes no mistakes."

AN OMNISCIENT FATHER

Is your God an all-wise Father, who knows the end from the beginning, who knows all the causes and all the outcomes, and who never makes a mistake? We may pray for something that seems very good to us, but God knows the "what ifs" in our lives. He knows the calamities that might occur if He answered our prayers in the way we think best. He also knows about all our difficult situations and wants to turn them into something tremendously good.

This view of God as an omniscient Father comes into focus very clearly as the years pass. One of the advantages of growing older is that we can look back and see that God has not made a single mistake in our lives. Maybe we'll have to get to heaven before we understand some things, but it's exciting to recognize as the years come and go that God has worked everything for good if we have really loved Him. When we keep a record of what is happening to us, it isn't long before we realize that the difficult things are there for a reason, and God is making no mistakes.

PRAY REQUESTS—NOT ANSWERS

When we first started a telephone prayer chain in our church, I, as chairman, soon learned that it was a full-time job. With sixty-six pray-ers signing up and averaging four, five, sometimes six prayer requests per day, it became more than I, as a pastor's wife, had time to handle, and so I turned over the chairmanship to another woman. When Elmy took over I said to her, "Some people will be calling to give you answers instead of requests. When they ask you to pray that such and such will happen, tell them kindly, 'We do not pray answers, we pray requests.'"

Do you see the difference? When we pray answers, we're demanding that God do something and we're telling Him we want it done now—"just the way we want it, Lord." When we're bringing our requests to Him, we're saying, "Lord, here's the need"—the circumstance, the person, whatever it may be; then we ask Him to answer according to His omniscient will.

Even with pure motives, it's easy to pray answers rather than requests. One woman on a prayer chain to which I belong is a returned missionary to Africa. After she and her family came back to the States, they all wished they were back on the field, so they started to pray, "Lord, send us back to Africa." They even reapplied for their position.

One day I received a telephone call from this dear lady. She was sobbing. "Ev, we just received word from our mission board that the position we held is filled, and we can't go back. Oh, Ev, we prayed and prayed that God would send us back to Africa."

What could I say about her praying that beautiful, noble "answer" to God? "Honey," I comforted, "you prayed the wrong prayer. If God had wanted you back on your mission station, He could have kept that position open until your letter arrived. It must not have been His will."

A PAWN IN GOD'S HANDS?

I was discussing this with a faculty wife one day, and she said, "Look, Girl, I'd feel like a pawn in God's hand if I ever prayed that way."

I thought for a minute. *Wow! Maybe so.* Then I said, "You know, maybe the greatest privilege in the whole world would be for me to be a pawn in the hands of God, a pawn who never makes a mistake. Just think, I'd never have to 'trial and error' anything. I'd never fall on my face (which I do very frequently). If God were in control of my every action, I would never do anything wrong. What a privilege to be a pawn in God's hands!"

But God hasn't quite chosen to do things that way, has He? God has given me a free will, and He has given you a free will. He has given us the privilege of saying, "All right, Lord, I'm free. I have a free will, but I want to do what You know is not a mistake in my life." Then, it isn't God pushing Evelyn, is it?

I'm not being a pawn on a chessboard if I say willingly, "Lord, I really don't know what the best approach would be, where I should go, when I should start." With my free will I can say, "Now, Lord, You know all the 'what ifs' and all the outcomes. So, Lord, in my free will, You just use me to bring about Your perfect will on Planet Earth."

ARE YOU ASKING AMISS?

How can we be sure that we are not asking amiss? James writes, "Ye ask, and receive not, because ye ask amiss, that ye may consume it upon your lusts" (James 4:3). Let's never insult God by saying, "O Lord, that other woman's husband looks just a little bit good to me. Is it okay if I just sit at his feet—in my imagination? There won't be anything physical about our relationship, Lord." Let's not ever ask whether that can be God's will. We know what His will is, for He says, "Be ye holy for I am holy."

Perhaps we say, "Lord, *look* at that new car, that new house," or "Wow! Look at her wardrobe, Lord! Is it all right if I'm just a little bit jealous?" Now, we don't really ask God such questions, but we often rationalize our feelings and attitudes in an attempt to justify them, don't we?

It may be that we're a little bit touchy. We whimper and complain, "Lord, she rubs me the wrong way. Look at what she did. I really don't like her very well. Could that be Your will, Lord?" No. God's Word says, "Love does not demand its own way. It is not irritable or touchy" (1 Corinthians 13:5, TLB). So one sure way of not asking amiss is to know God's Word, the Bible. If God calls it sin, don't insult Him by asking about it.

But the Bible isn't all negative. We find in God's Word what we *can* do and what we *ought* to do. Responding to the positive commands of God's Word is another prerequisite to answered prayer based on obedience: "If ye abide in Me, and My words abide in you, ye shall ask what ye will and it shall be done unto you" (John 15:7). There is nothing in God's Word that is contrary to God's will. If we find it in His Word, we can believe it, we can live it, and we can act upon it,

At this point you may be asking, "Do we dare to

pray for somebody's salvation? Is it God's will?" Peter tells us, "The Lord is . . . not willing that any should perish" (2 Peter 3:9). We are to pray for those outside the body of Christ, but we must not forget that the person for whom we are praying has a free will, just as you and I have. God never superimposes His will upon anyone, but the timing and the sovereignty are His. Pray, yes. It is God's will that we pray that everyone will be saved, but we are to leave the results with God.

There is one more way we can be sure we don't ask amiss. God's Word tells us we believers have two Intercessors—Christ at the right hand of God and the Holy Spirit dwelling in us. The Holy Spirit takes the prayers *when we don't know what we should pray for as we ought* and brings them to the Father *"according to the will of God"* (Romans 8:26-27). At those times when we cannot even put the deep yearnings of our hearts into words, we can rest assured that the Holy Spirit is interceding for us before the throne of God according to the Father's will.

WHEN GOD SAYS NO

Is it ever good when God says no? I had a meaningful no answer when we first moved to St. Paul. I was asked to be the vice-president of a large hospital auxiliary. I knew nothing about the two hospitals they served, but was assured it was a "You-won't-have-to-do-a-thing" job.

I immediately called back home to the prayer chains I had just left, asking them to pray for God's will. Soon the answer came from them and from others I had asked to pray: "God is saying no." And He was telling me no also.

When I told the committee what God had said, I almost felt the eyebrows being raised in surprise. I could not understand either why God would say no to such a great job when I was lonely with nothing to do in my new town.

A couple of weeks later, I found out why. The auxiliary president's husband was transferred out of state. Within two weeks, I would have been president of an organization that ran coffee shops and gift shops, and supervised volunteers and student candy stripers in two large hospitals. In addition, the whole work was needing to be reorganized—a process which was completed four years later. What a mess I would have made of that job!

"O dear God," I prayed, "thank You for knowing the 'what ifs' and for keeping me from falling on my face."

IS SUFFERING EVER GOD'S WILL?

One year in our neighborhood Bible study we discovered a verse of Scripture which had a great impact on all of our lives. I knew the concept was scriptural, but I had never noticed it in God's Word before. "Wherefore let them that suffer according to the will of God commit the keeping of their souls to Him in well doing, as unto a faithful Creator" (1 Peter 4:19).

Those who suffer according to God's will—is that in the Bible? Yes, it is. And almost everyone in our group that year was suffering. Of course, they weren't suffering because they were in the Bible study group (I hope). They were suffering in their bodies and in their spirits in various ways, but they began to see tremendous things take place. Whenever a problem arose, God would give us a specific answer immediately in His Word, and we would receive strength, grace, peace, maturity in Christ—whatever was needed.

The husband of one woman in that group had peculiar fungus growing under his skull, and his only hope for survival was a drug that had side effects in the mind and personality. He became an entirely different person. As a result he divorced his wife and turned his back on his whole family. Recently, I had lunch with this woman. She's still radiant in Christ.

Another member's husband had contracted syphilis and had to name all his partners—a whole string of them. His wife found strength in the Word of God.

Two daughters of one woman, both teenagers, were pregnant out of wedlock, as was the teenage daughter of another woman. About the least that happened to anybody was major surgery or breast cancer!

Can suffering be God's will? Yes, we all saw it come into focus in 1 Peter. If you're suffering read that epistle. It's tremendous. We, as Christians, aren't promised that we'll be free from suffering. Sometimes we suffer simply because we have frail, human bodies, but if we're committed to the God who doesn't ever make a mistake, we can have the assurance that He has permitted our suffering and *has a specific reason for it*.

If you are suffering as you read this chapter, can you truly pray, "Lord, I still want Your will. Amen"? It means taking every facet, every area of your life, and turning it over to the Lord. It's easy to pray, "Lord, how I love Your will" when we're on the mountaintop. But there are other times when we can only pray, "O Lord, I'm in the valley and it hurts. But, Lord, my answer is yes. I know that Your will is right, and I'm willing to conform to Your will, no matter what it is."

ALL THINGS FOR GOOD

Way back in our college days, I faced a crisis when I lost my third pregnancy. I had already had a miscarriage, then a full-term stillborn, and now another miscarriage. "Lord, Lord, why all of this?" my heart cried.

It was just after World War II, and we had returned to college. In a burning bomber over Berlin, Chris had promised God that he would become a preacher after the war was over. Then God allowed us to lose this third baby. Was He turning His back and letting us suffer?

No, not at all. At that time God gave me Romans 8:28, "And we know that all things work together for good to those that love God." I loved God and Chris loved Him, and God had His reasons for not allowing those three babies to live.

What all of God's reasons were I may never know, short of eternity. But one thing God seemed to tell me was, "Do you think that you and Chris could have gone through seven more years of schooling if you had had those three babies? Your dad had become an invalid and Chris' dad had died leaving two younger children. Could you have had the courage and the financial support to face seven more years of schooling with three babies to care for?"

Did God make a mistake? No. Not at all. Romans 8:28 has been our family's life verse ever since. We know that *all* things, absolutely everything, work together for our good. This was the omniscient God who never makes a mistake dealing in the lives of those who loved Him.

Despite my earlier miscarriages, Jan came along normally, and then, when we were in our first pastorate, it seemed God was giving us a second healthy child. But Judy lived to be only seven months old. And all the pain came back again. "Lord, how come? Haven't I suffered enough? Haven't I learned?"

When God took Judy, He spoke to me so clearly from the twelfth chapter of Hebrews: "For they [our earthly fathers] verily for a few days chastened us after their own pleasure; but He [God] *for our profit*, that we might be partakers of His holiness" (v. 10). God said, "Evelyn, this is for your profit. If you're going to be a pastor's wife, you will have to understand some of these things." I wish I could write of all the ways that God through the years has used that experience for my profit as I've stood with heartbroken parents by tiny caskets or hospital cribs.

Ultimately God did permit us to raise three happy, healthy children, Jan, Nancy, and Kurt. And

He had things to teach us through them, as well as through those we lost.

Do we ever arrive? My mother-in-law once said to me, "Oh, Evelyn, I'm over seventy and I still haven't arrived." No, we never arrive, but God is doing something. He's making us what He wants us to be. It's in the suffering and in the hard things that He wants us to say, "Lord, You never make a mistake. I want only Your will."

When I was speaking about this at an After Five Club near my home, three young women came to speak to me. I learned that one of them was going blind, one had just lost her two-year-old son in an accident, and the other was facing serious hip surgery within the next few days. As they spoke to me individually, each said that Romans 8:28 had come into focus for her that night. And each added, "I am now willing for God's will, whatever it may be."

THE OTHER HALF OF GOD'S WILL

In the previous chapter I wrote about the open door and the excitement. That's half of it, but the other half is being willing for God's will no matter how hard it is. At one of our church circle meetings, our spiritual life chairman, whose only sister was dying of cancer, said while leading our devotions, "I have struggled for months and months. Now I can finally tell you that if God takes my sister or lets her live, I am willing for His will."

We forgot everything else and started to pray. There were women there with very serious problems.

A young, pregnant mother who had lost her only child to crib death the preceding March could say, "I'm willing for God's will in this pregnancy." Another lady suffering from Hodgkin's disease could say the same. Each of those women prayed and meant it, "Lord, I'm willing for Your will!" Then they immediately went to intercessory prayer for me while I spoke at the church where the youth pastor later said to me, "You turned our church upside down!"

If you and I want to be powerful intercessory pray-ers, we must be willing for God's will not only in the things for which we are praying—that's only half of it. The other half is *being willing for God's will in our own personal lives.*

HOT FIRES

At Lindon Karo's funeral, my fourteen-year-old niece was sobbing out her heartbreak; she loved her pastor dearly. As I put my arms around her, I said, "Carla, God must have something very, very great for you if He's giving you this hot a fire so early in life." What did I mean? I meant that God has a way of making us greater persons by the "hot fires" which are preparing us for what is ahead. This is a beautiful concept. David understood it. He said, "Thou hast enlarged me when I was in distress" (Psalm 4:1). The word *enlarged* means "prepared for the task ahead."

Our Jan learned this when she was in the ninth grade. Her friend Dave was a fantastic boy, an A student, president of the student council, as well as class president. He was captain of the basketball team, and had single-handedly pitched the local pony league baseball team to the world championship. His poetry had been published nationally—everything was going for him with two exceptions: Dave was not a Christian, and he had leukemia. But he didn't know about the leukemia and neither did Jan.

In the spring of that year, our local churches sponsored a gigantic youth rally with Dave Wilkerson as the speaker. At first Jan was timid about inviting Dave, but she finally worked up courage. On the evening of the rally, Chris and I drove them down to the armory. My husband sat close enough to Dave to hear him pray as he slipped to his knees at the end of the service: "Dear God, forgive all my sins and, Jesus, come into my heart as my Lord and Savior."

Dave had no idea at that time that he was soon to enter into battle with a deadly killer—leukemia. By the time the junior high yearbooks came out, Dave knew he was very sick, but hardly realized how near the end was. He wrote in Jan's yearbook: "Dear Jan, Thank you for introducing me to Christ. You'll never know what He means to me now, and what He will mean in the future."

Two weeks later, Dave's "future with Christ" was a reality. Early on the day he died, I was sitting alone in my purple chair in the living room. Sensing that something was wrong, Jan got out of bed, came downstairs and asked, "Where's Dad?"

"He's at Dave's house, Honey."

"Dave's gone, isn't he?"

"Yes."

For a little while we sat and cried together in that

little purple chair. I said, "Honey, God is making you finer gold." She had heard that many times in our home. We talked about Romans 8:28, and Job's assurance, "When He hath tried me, I shall come forth as gold" (Job 23:10). That morning I said to Jan what I had told Carla at Lindon Karo's funeral, "Honey, God must have something great in mind for you to give you all this 'fire' at your age." Then Jan sobbed, "Oh, Mother, what if I hadn't invited him to hear Dave Wilkerson preach?"

Dave's funeral was the largest that had ever been held in our city. Hundreds of teenagers, teachers, and school officials were present at the mortuary. As my husband stood up to speak, he said, " I can almost hear the basketball bouncing in heaven today." Then he told the people what Dave had said just before he died. He had raised himself from his bed and asked, "Where am I?"

His mother replied, "Dave, you're in Billings Hospital in Chicago and you're very, very sick. But all the doctors and nurses are here."

Then Dave had said, "Oh, no. Where I am it's all green and beautiful." And then he died.

My husband could tell all those teenagers and adults that Dave was with his Christ in a future that was only two weeks away when he had written about it in Jan's yearbook.

Suffering can be according to God's will. Are you willing—even if suffering is to be a part of your future?

COMMITTED TO HIS WILL

At our seminar session on this subject we invite participants at prayer time to commit their lives to God's perfect will. On a Wednesday morning, following such a session, one woman who attended committed her whole life, everything she held dear, to God's will. That very weekend her husband was killed in a motorboat accident! On the following Wednesday, one of the seminar members came with a message from the widow. "Please tell Evelyn that God prepared me for this experience when I committed my life to Him for His will last Wednesday."

Several months later at a prayer leaders' workshop, with tears in her eyes, she told us that she could really see God's will in this tragedy because one of her daughters who had turned away from Christ and left home had come back to Him, and was now taking her Daddy's place in leading the smaller children in Bible reading and prayer each day.

After prayer time in a seminar the following February, a young woman whose husband was a seminary student said to me, "I cannot pray for God's will in my life. I cannot do it."

When I asked why, she replied, "I prayed and prayed and prayed for a baby. Then I became pregnant and was so excited, because I knew it was an answer to prayer. I knew God had given us that baby! But last December I had a miscarriage—and now I don't have my baby."

I said. "God doesn't make mistakes. He gave you the child for just the few months that you carried it. God had accomplished His purpose for that baby's life."

The young woman thought for a moment, and said, "Now I can pray for God's will." We bowed our heads and she prayed, "Lord, I want only Your will in my life."

Following another seminar session on God's will, a young man who had undergone surgery for a brain tumor about five years previously struggled up the aisle with the help of two canes, and asked if he could say something. We all thought he was going to ask for prayer for healing or make some other request. But, supported on either side by his "new" mother and myself, he leaned toward to the microphone and said, "I just want to thank God for these seminars and for the privilege of being here. You know, my mother died while I was still in a coma after my accident." (He called his brain tumor his accident.) Then he added, "If all these things hadn't happened, I would not have come to live with this new mother who is a Christian. She has introduced me to Jesus, and I have received Him as my Savior. If I hadn't had my accident, I would never have come to know Jesus." Then he said, "I'm willing for anything that God's will has for me." He stood there, not able to support himself, willing for God's will.

THE PLACE OF PRAISE

We may reach the place suddenly, or it may take us years to realize that God isn't making a mistake in our lives. But then we are at the point where we can praise Him. A new Christian in my Bible study called me one day and said, "Mrs. Chris, I think I found a wrong translation in the Bible. It's there in the first chapter of James, verses 2 to 4. Isn't it wrong when it says, 'Count it all joy when you fall into various trials'?"

I smiled over the phone and said, "No, Honey, it's not wrong. This is the place you reach when after years and years of trials and difficulties, you see that all has been working out for your good, and that God's will is perfect. You see that He has made no mistakes. He knew all of the 'what ifs' in your life. When you finally recognize this, even *during* the trials, it's possible to have joy, deep down joy."

Philippians 4:6 comes into focus at this point: "Be careful [anxious] for nothing; but in everything, by prayer and supplication with *thanksgiving*, let your requests be made known unto God." It is a privilege to see God being glorified in our lives. We are to give thanks always, knowing that we have a God who never makes a mistake. And if we are going to be effectual intercessory pray-ers, praying in the will of God, it's not something we tack on to the end of our prayers. It's a commitment to God's will, a way of life. It's being willing for His will in the things for which we are praying and in our personal lives. And it's "giving thanks always for *all* things unto God and the Father in the name of our Lord Jesus Christ" (Ephesians 5:20). As I said earlier, this is easier said than done—but the rewards are fantastic!

For you to do:

1. *Think of the most important thing in the world to you. (It may be health, a loved one, a job, finances, schooling, etc.)*
2. *Now pray: Father, I want Your will in this thing that is most important in the world to me.*
3. *Now in prayer thank God for however He chooses to answer, knowing it is according to His perfect will.*
4. *Please don't pray the following prayer unless you really mean it: Father, I want Your will in every area of my life including my job, my home, my health, my children, my loved ones, and my service for You. Amen.*

THE SPACE DIMENSION OF PRAYER—
WHERE WE PRAY

But thou, when thou prayest, enter into thy closet, and when thou hast shut the door, pray to thy Father which is in secret; and thy Father which seeth in secret shall reward thee openly. Matthew 6:6

y old green chair has long since been reupholstered, but years ago, when it was brand new, it became the quiet place to which I would steal very early in the morning to spend time alone with God. It was on my knees at that old chair that I would pour out the inmost groanings of my heart—for only God to hear. Groanings much too personal to be heard by any other. My tears stained its cushion as I knelt interceding for a loved one. It was there I was filled with awe and adoration for Him and all He is—the "heaven of heavens cannot contain Thee" (1 Kings 8:27).

It was there on my knees with my open Bible that God taught me to wait on Him for every point in a series of messages. It was there with my head buried in my hands that I begged God for wisdom for a certain message that I was to give. Not getting any answers, I reached for the morning newspaper, laid it on the seat of the chair, and read in the headlines that Russia had sent Sputnik I into outer space. Then God said, "It isn't who can *conquer* outer space that counts but He who *created* it and by whom it consists" (see Colossians 1:16-17). I had my message!

PRIVATE PRAYER—PUBLIC PRAYING

Do you have a secret place for private prayer, a certain corner, a particular chair, or a room set apart where you can spend time alone with God? A "closet" where you daily *shut the door* to pray to your Father in secret? The group concept of prayer is important, and we do need to pray *with* one another, "not forsaking the assembling of ourselves together" (see Hebrews 10:25). But the drawing apart to pray in secret is perhaps the most vital type of prayer in which we engage. It is also an indicator of the kind of prayer group participant we really are, for *it is our private praying that determines the quality and validity of our public praying.*

Though we are never to be critical of the prayers of others, we can often recognize in our prayer groups those who have spent time in private closet prayer and the others who have come perhaps to do the only praying that they have done all week. Some struggle and strain to sound pious, but it's obvious that they haven't experienced the deeper dimension of closet prayer.

Have you ever seen a bright blue iceberg? In Alaska I stared in awe at a mountain lake filled with beautiful blue icebergs that had broken off Portage Glacier. Immediately my mind went back to an article in a *Family Tie* magazine that compared our secret praying to an iceberg. The "Absolutely No Boating" sign on the edge of the lake reminded me that eight-ninths of the bulk of an iceberg is below the water-line—out of sight. Only one-ninth is visible above the surface. The next day at our prayer seminar in Anchorage I explained how prayer should be like those icebergs, with about one-ninth showing in our public group praying and eight-ninths out of sight in our secret closets.

OTHER CLOSETS

I can almost hear you saying, "I can't spend great periods of my time in a closet." No, neither can I, but I have found another kind of closet praying. It's just drawing apart to God wherever I am—at the kitchen sink, at a desk, or even in a room filled with people.

"You must have tremendous power of concentration," someone said.

No, I've just learned to draw apart from people to God. Practicing this at a California retreat with 525 people packed in a room that barely held 500, we found, though touching elbows physically, that we could each draw apart mentally to God. This too is closet praying, though it is no substitute for drawing apart to that one spot, at that one time of the day, when we really spend time with God and His Word.

One of my very favorite "closets" is my car. As I draw apart, you may be sure I don't take my hands off the wheel, fold them, and kneel. To shut my eyes would be even worse!

One morning as I was getting ready to leave for an all-day prayer seminar fifty miles away, everything went wrong. My husband called from California asking me to find out when he was to meet certain professors at the San Francisco airport and to give the information to his secretary so he could call her after I had gone. I couldn't find the professors, I couldn't find the secretary, after frantically dialing all the possible numbers.

Then my son called from school, "Mom, I forgot all my books; could you bring them over?" I did, and was completely out of time when I left his school, only to run into such a long detour that I could hardly find my way back to the freeway.

As I finally emerged on the right road, I cried to God. "O Lord, take over! Remove from me all this tension and frustration. Flow through me with Your peace and power. Make me what You want me to be by the time I arrive at the prayer seminar." And He did! My car had become my prayer closet.

Even a plane seat can be a prayer closet. For two years I had been praying with a friend about her sister who did not know Christ. Every time my friend wrote to her sister, she'd call asking me to pray for God to work in her heart as she received the letter. One day my plane had a ten minute layover in a Midwestern city with no time to disembark. I looked out over the city and thought, "That's where my friend's sister lives!" Suddenly there descended from God a heavy, overwhelming burden to pray for her. I sat in that plane in the very depths of intercessory prayer. Two days later my elated friend called to say, "I just received a letter from my sis, and she accepted Christ!" When? The exact day God had said in that plane, "Evelyn, pray."

WHICH POSTURE?

Just as our momentary closet praying requires no particular place, neither does it require a certain prayer posture. In one of seminars a man announced to me after the first session that he would not be back. "You're not praying scripturally," he said. When I asked him to please explain, he replied, "You're not 'holding up holy hands.' " He could see only this one position to be used at all times, even though I pointed out to him that there are many postures of prayer mentioned in the Word of God.

When Jesus was praying in the Garden of Gethsemane, He gave us the example of *kneeling* in prayer. "And He was withdrawn from them about a stone's cast, and kneeled down, and prayed" (Luke 22:41). At the tomb of Lazarus, while standing, "Jesus *lifted up His eyes*, and said, 'Father, I thank Thee that Thou hast heard Me.' " (John 11:41). Paul wrote, "I will therefore that men pray everywhere, *lifting up holy hands*, without wrath and doubting" (1 Timothy 2:8).

My husband can recall circumstances in which men experienced such grief and anguish that they lay prostrate on the floor of his study. One was a dad who had just learned that his teenage daughter was pregnant out of wedlock. He cast himself to the floor, weeping, and my husband had to take him in his arms and gently lift him up.

King Solomon, in the Old Testament, *prostrated himself before the Lord* when he prayed in the temple. His father, David, communed with God upon his bed (Psalm 4:4). Whatever our posture, wherever the place, the ears of our God are open to our cry (see Psalm 34:15).

HOLY PLACES

God does not dwell in temples made with hands. Even so, some spots have been used as closets for prayer by so many that they seem to be holy places. Have you ever stepped into a room and felt God there? My husband and I were looking over the grounds at a Midwestern retreat center one fall. We stepped into an old chapel—and I felt God's presence immediately. "Hon, please go on without me for a few minutes," I said. I knelt at that altar—not talking or praying, but just *feeling* God so powerfully there.

Another time I arrived at Bethel Seminary in St. Paul to speak at a women's retreat just as the planning committee stepped out of the Eric Frykenberg Prayer Tower, where they had been praying. Their eyes were wide with wonder and amazement. "We felt Jesus in there!"

"Yes," I replied, "that is one of those places where I always feel a particular sense of the presence of Christ." That little circular room has no windows or furniture, but it is filled with the thousands of prayers uttered by students and faculty of that seminary—and His presence!

Christ recognized the need for spending time alone with God. What a tremendous example Christ's prayer life was to His followers and to us. Though the disciples were Jesus' very closest friends, He knew there were times He had to pray in secret to His Heavenly Father. Although Christ taught His disciples the concept of group prayer, as we have learned in previous chapters, He also knew the importance of this private closet praying. Even though He Himself was God incarnate, He thought it necessary to withdraw to a mountain to pray all night before the important task of choosing the 12 Apostles. If He, why not us?

For you to pray:

Lord, give me the joy of secret closet praying. Keep me faithful to shut the door every day and spend time with You and Your Word in secret. Teach me to draw apart alone with You, no matter where I am or with whom.

The Time Dimension of Prayer— When We Pray

Pray without ceasing. 1 Thessalonians 5:17

*D*id you ever sit in a room before a glowing fire with someone you love? Did you talk every minute? Or did you feel compelled every now and then to clear your throat and say, "Now, dear, I think I'll say something to you." Then with a bright introduction, did you proceed with a formal speech? Of course not. When you're with a person you love, there need not be a bit of conversation in order for you to experience real communication. If you feel like saying something, you do; if not, you don't; but the line of communication is always open.

Praying without ceasing is like that. How? It's simply turning the dial of our communication system with God to *On*, making possible a two-way conversation with Him at any time. When that communication line is open, we can say whatever we want to Him, and He in turn can say anything He wishes to us. Yes, it's possible to "pray without ceasing" twenty-four hours a day.

When we leave our daily closet praying, do we walk out and slam the door, saying, "That's it for today. Same time tomorrow, Lord, same station"? That isn't what the Holy Spirit meant when He inspired Paul to write, "Pray without ceasing"

(1 Thessalonians 5:17). Nor is it what Christ meant when He taught His disciples, "Men ought always to pray, and not to faint" (Luke 18:1).

After Paul lists the armor with which we are to resist Satan he goes on to say, "Praying *always* with all prayer and supplication in the Spirit" (Ephesians 6:18). The source of strength in our battle with the enemy is "praying always." But when the line of communication with God closes, wham—the fiery darts of Satan strike! But that need not be the case. Let's break down the day and see how the communication system between God and us can be open all twenty-four hours.

A LARK OR AN OWL?

How do you start your day? Are you lark or an owl? Larks twitter and sing in the morning, but by the end of the day they're not doing too well, they have slowed down considerably. Owls take a little longer to get going in the morning—"Right now I don't love anybody, but when I start loving again, you'll be first on the list." But owls gain momentum as the night progresses.

We're divided at our house. I'm a lark and my husband is definitely an owl. When we pray together at night and Chris prays on and on, I sometimes have to say, "Hurry up, Chris; you're losing me." But in the morning it's a different story. Chris groans and pulls the covers up tighter when I shake him to tell him some great gem that I've just gotten from the Lord.

Because our individual, built-in clocks function

differently, I've learned that there are no spiritual brownie points for being a lark. Is it possible our Heavenly Father created some of us to be larks and some to be owls so He would have somebody on the alert all twenty-four hours of the day?

I used to say, and I'm sure it was with pride, "I'm creative in the morning. That is my creative time." Then I realized, "Ev, you're not creative in the morning; you've just learned to listen to God in the wee hours."

When I'm asked, "How do you get all those messages ready? How can you possibly write so many?" I have to reply, "I don't write messages, but I keep a little notebook on my bedstand at all times. Then lying there communing with my Heavenly Father early in the morning, I just jot down whatever He says to me."

When I awaken, I say, "Lord, here I am. What do You want to say to me?" I usually think they should be ideas for immediate needs, but frequently He gives thoughts for retreats and messages months away. I write them down and keep them in file folders. Then when I put those papers in outline form, it's astounding to learn that God has given me every single thought I'll ever need—in time!

It's a very exciting procedure to wait upon God early in the morning while my mind is fresh, before anyone else comes on the scene, or before the "tyranny of the urgent" rushes in. Have you learned to say in the morning, "Lord, here I am. You tell me what You want me to know today, what You want me to do"? Have you asked Him, "Is there someone You want me to call? What do You have in mind for me today?" You'll be amazed at His answers!

One morning as I was lying in bed talking to the Lord, I said, as I frequently do, "Okay, Lord, who would You have me call on the phone today?" The answer came as if it were in lights, "Mona."

"But, Lord, I don't know Mona. I met her at a band concert, and a PTA meeting—and that's it."

I waited until the kids left for school; then I went to the phone and said, "Lord, You're going to have to tell me what to say to Mona—I don't know."

I really felt a little silly about calling her, but I dialed and said, "Good morning, Mona. This is Evelyn Christenson from down the street." That's all I said. And Mona started to cry. She told me that the day before, she and her husband had been told by the doctors that their son, Dave (our Jan's friend), had leukemia and would never recover. My obedience gave me the opportunity to at least build a bridge to Mona and to comfort her in her distress.

One morning, after my daughter had asked me to pray for a girl who was feuding with her parents, I said, "Lord, if You want me to talk to her, have her call or come over." At 2 o'clock in the afternoon I answered my doorbell, and there she stood with a suitcase in her hand. "Hi, I've come to move in with you for awhile."

It had been one of those unbelievably hectic days, and I glanced heavenward and sighed, "Lord, I didn't mean that *literally*."

I used to think that if one were an owl, talking with God in the morning wasn't necessary. But one day, as I was reading Psalm 5, I saw something for the first time. I said to Chris, "Hey, it's really scriptural to talk to God first thing in the morning." In all the times I had read that psalm, it had never really hit me before.

> Give ear to my words, O Lord, consider my meditation. Hearken unto the voice of my cry, my King, and my God: for unto Thee will I pray. My voice shalt Thou hear in the morning, O Lord; in the morning will I direct my prayer unto Thee, and will look up (Psalm 5:1-3).

It doesn't say that hours of prayer time are necessary, but at least we must say Good Morning to the Lord and give Him our day. So whether you are a lark or an owl, God's Word says early in the morning, before the tyranny of the urgent, before breakfast, before the school buses, before anyone says a word to you, "Early in the morning, Lord, I will look up, and pray unto You."

PRAYER BEFORE SCHOOL

After breakfast, it's time for the children to start off to school. Since our first child was in kindergarten, we have made a practice in our home of praying individually with each of our children just as they left for school. For me, this has been a very precious experience. It has been more than a time to pray! We have been able to put our arms around our children, assuring them of the security of their home, and then to send them out into the big, often overwhelming world with God watching over them, whatever they will face that day.

Every once in a while I'm told by my son, "Hurry up, Mom, make it short. The school bus is coming," and out the door he goes! Sometimes it's only one or two sentences. But meeting God with our family before we separate is a very vital part of our day.

THE DAY PROGRESSES

I have a great time with the Lord in the morning. As God and I communicate with one another, He tells me what He wants me to do, and I say, "All right, Lord." There are no problems. There aren't any people around to bother me. There are no bad reactions for me to contend with. You know, I could really be a tremendous Christian if I could stay in my closet with God. But I can't stay there all day. I can't even remain sheltered with members of my own family, those who love me. I have to get out and meet people—and occasionally my early morning relationship with God suddenly falls apart!

I'm a people person, and I really like almost everybody I meet. But once in a while somebody makes me bristle, and I retaliate. There are other occasions when I just look at someone and think, "Oh, brother!"

How do I solve the problem? I've learned what I call my *SOS prayer*. I say, "Help, Lord." (But not out loud!) "Lord, give me the attitude *You* want me to have toward that person."

Perhaps you can imagine what it's like for a wife and mother to prepare to go out of town for a speaking engagement. You get all the laundry done, matching the socks with the shirts. Then you stock the refrigerator with enough food for all the days you'll be gone, outline each of your messages, try to get yourself and your clothes ready, and do the last-minute shopping. It's really hectic! In addition, you have to get "prayed up." You just can't go without spiritual preparation, so you spend extra time with the Lord. Finally you settle into the plane seat, review your notes once more, and pray.

Things had gone that way before I arrived in an Eastern city for a retreat a few years ago. As I was being introduced to the ladies, a pastor's wife who was sitting next to me leaned over and gibed, almost sneering, "Do you really like these little women's meetings?"

Wow! After all I'd gone through to get there! Besides, I didn't think that meeting was so little—about 200 women were there from several states. And I was all primed and ready to share what the Lord had given me for them. Do you know what I did? I bristled!

Now, I didn't have time to say a long prayer—I had only seconds left before speaking. As I walked to the platform, I silently pleaded with the Lord, "*Help, SOS*, give me the attitude You want me to have toward that pastor's wife." And do you know, all the bristle disappeared. Because God knew I didn't have a lot of time to get this cleared up, He answered my SOS prayer just like *that*! What would have happened if I had started out bristling at that audience? It would have pulled the rug right out from under the whole retreat.

One of the prayer requests presented at a faculty wives' prayer meeting I attended involved a serious financial problem. On the day before the prayer meeting, the promise of a large gift of money for the new campus had been withdrawn, and now we were going to pray about it.

As we were drinking coffee and chatting before the start of the prayer meeting, a woman came in whom I had never met. I didn't know who she was, but I looked down my spiritual nose and thought, "My word, she's the squarest woman I've ever seen in my life." And the more she talked, the more square I thought she was.

Then the Lord began to reprove me, "Evelyn, that's sin." Do you remember our first prerequisite to answered prayer? "If I regard iniquity in my heart, the Lord will not hear me." I suddenly realized that I was about to spend my morning in prayer for these financial needs with sin in *my* heart! Another SOS prayer flew to heaven, "Lord, please give me the attitude You want me to have toward that woman, whoever she is."

You know, when we pray that prayer, we never ask amiss. God knows what attitude He wants to give us. When we look at Christ's life, we can see that sometimes His perfect attitude was love, sometimes it was righteous indignation, sometimes patience, sometimes discipline, sometimes compassion.

That day God gave me a surprise. Guess who prayed first at that prayer meeting? She did. And as she started to pray, I suddenly realized that this woman had a dimension to her prayer life that I knew nothing about. She said, "Thank You, Lord, that that money didn't come through yesterday." She went on, "Now, Lord, You have given us the *privilege* of being on our faces before You this morning with a desperate need. Lord, what a privilege this is. Thank You, Lord. And thank You that today the school's president has the privilege of being on his face before You with his need. Thank You that the whole staff has this tremendous need, and thank You that they have the privilege of being on their faces before You."

I felt two inches high.

When I learned who this woman was, I discovered some other things. She had an intercessory prayer life that was never less than two hours a day. She used a prayer list that was pages and pages long, containing the names of the people for whom she prayed daily. And *I* had looked at *her* and thought, "Wow, is she square!"

I had a trying experience when I was teaching wives during a pastors' conference. We had gone over the material on praying in God's will, and were going to have a spiritual exercise by each of us taking partners with whom we would share and pray. My partner was a young pastor's wife. We took our chairs to a corner and got all ready for the spiritual exercise, when suddenly she looked me right in the eye and said, "I hate you."

Do you think I smiled and said, "Oh, I just love you"? Not on your life. I said, "I guess we had better not do our exercise; we'd better just talk. Tell me why you hate me."

But as I was talking outwardly, inwardly I was

praying, "SOS, Lord. Help me to have the attitude You want me to have toward this person." And God gave me the ability to sit there calmly without becoming angry and retaliating. "Would you like to tell me why you hate me?" I asked.

She said, "Okay, I'll tell you. My husband has been interviewed by the pulpit committee seeking a pastor for your former church." She went on, "I didn't know who you were when I came to this meeting. I had never seen you before, had never heard one of your tapes, but I knew you were the wife of the former pastor of that church." Then she exploded, "You're everything I don't want to be and can't be in a pastor's wife, so I hate you. Look at that dress you're wearing," she said. "I'm a sweatshirt-and-jeans girl myself."

I was at a loss as to where to start, but God seemed to be saying to share deeply with her out of my heart. I told her of the hard things I had talked about in my message that morning, things that had happened *during* my time at that church. I even told her of a very personal trial I never mention in public, and how those wonderful people prayed for me— just as they would pray for her if she were their pastor's wife. It wasn't long before the two of us were in tears, clasping hands, and praying together.

As we parted, she said, "As my husband and I drive home this afternoon, I want to tell him about how I feel now. Will you pray for me?"

I said I would, but she didn't wait until afternoon. At lunch her husband came flying across the dining room and asked, "What did you do to my wife?"

I told him I didn't do anything to his wife, but I wanted to know what happened.

He said, "You know, God is calling me to leave the church I'm now serving, and my wife has been saying, 'Absolutely not. I don't care where you're called. I won't go.' But she just came to me and said, 'Honey, wherever God leads you, I'll go along.' What did you do?"

What had I done? I had prayed, "SOS, Lord. Give me the right attitude toward this woman." And immediately He had given me an understanding attitude toward a young pastor's wife who didn't want to leave her rural community and her sweatshirts and jeans.

Not long ago a woman stopped me in a church and said, "We just called a new pastor." Guess who it was? That same young man! Then she went on, "Do you know why we called him? He's a great guy, but we were very impressed with his wife. She was so eager to have her husband where God wanted him to be, and she was undergirding his ministry like we've never seen any pastor's wife do before." I smiled and breathed a thank-you to God for that little sweat-shirt-and-jeans girl who only a year before had said, "I hate you."

When we say to God, "Give me the attitude You want me to have toward that person," immediately these amazing attitudes come, the ones He wants us to have. We don't have to reach for the pill bottle. I had one toddler who I said was not just an "*Anacin* headache kid," she was a "*Vanquish* headache kid." She could paint the back fence and her hair and everything else faster than I could get out there to grab the paint can! What do we do? We pray, "Lord, right now, give me the attitude You want me to have toward that person in my family, toward that person I meet on the street, even toward the one who looks at me and says, 'I hate you.'" All day long if people rub us the wrong way, we can have the communication system open between us and God. We just pray, "*SOS, Lord*. Give me the attitude *You* want me to have." It works all day long, the whole twenty-four hours.

BEAR ONE ANOTHER'S BURDENS—
ALL THE TIME

How about your family? Is it as easy for your children to say, "Mom, I'm having a math test at 10:30, please pray," as it is for them to ask you for $2.50 for lunch money? Do your children know that your communication system with God is always open?

One morning while she was still in high school, one of our daughters was so frightened about an upcoming important interview that I found her sick to her stomach in the bathroom. I helped her out the front door and promised to pray. Soon the phone rang. "Mother, it went great," she exclaimed, and then softly, "I could *feel* you praying, Mom."

Our married daughter's father-in-law had just had open-heart surgery. Suddenly the "Red Alert" was flashed over the hospital intercom. Jan ran to a phone, dialed our number and, with the sounds of running hospital personnel in the background, said,

"Mother, Skip's dad's heart has stopped." *My* heart stood still. I felt so helpless and so far away. "What can I do?" There was a long pause, and then she said, "Just pray, Mother, just pray," and hung up. I did pray, and her father-in-law revived and God gave him four more years to live. But the point is that Jan knew she could depend on me to pray about her concerns, any time, any place.

This family prayer support works two ways. After finishing a retreat at Mt. Hermon, California, I phoned home long distance. My then ten-year-old son answered with "How did it go, Mom?"

"Oh, Kurt, it went just great."

"Well," he said with pride in his voice, "how could you miss with my whole pastor's Saturday class praying for you?"

Do you have someone who will pray for you and for whom you will pray? If you don't know where to start with all these prayer suggestions, find one person with whom you can share the secret problems and needs of your life. Someone who cares and who will never, never divulge your secrets. Then fulfill the law of Christ by "bearing one another's burdens" (Galatians 6:2).

THE NIGHTWATCH

Are you one of these people whom God can awaken in the middle of the night to pray for one of His needs down here on Planet Earth? "But I need my sleep," you say. So did I, or at least I thought I did. For many years I was strictly hung up on sleeping pills—I thought I had to have eight solid hours of sleep or I'd never make it the next day. Then one summer day, I very undramatically tossed those pills into the toilet, flushed it, and said, "Lord, I'm not going to worry if I'm awake at night, because if You awaken me, there's a reason for it. I'll just ask You, 'For whom should I be praying?'"

God knows when I'm finished praying and ready to go back to sleep. And somehow there's no frustration and I never miss the sleep when God needs me to pray. It's a very beautiful and exciting experience.

One night the Lord awoke me and said, "Pray for Jacque" (a long-time prayer partner). At that time she was in San Francisco, and I learned later that she was going through a very deep spiritual battle, seemingly surrounded by forces of Satan. A letter Jacque wrote to me the next morning confirmed the reason God had awakened me. As I prayed in St. Paul, great peace had flooded her in San Francisco. *If at night you can't sleep, don't count sheep—talk to the Shepherd!*

Another time I was driving on a Wisconsin freeway very late on a Saturday night. It hadn't occurred to me that my gas tank might be a little bit hungry since I wasn't. All at once, *putt, putt, putt.* I was out of gas! I pulled off to the side of the road and opened the trunk (I knew that if I opened the hood, other motorists approaching from behind would see that there was a woman alone in a car).

As each set of headlights appeared behind me, I prayed, "Lord, if there's anybody in that car with whom I won't be safe, keep them going, Lord, keep them going." I sat there for fifteen minutes, and every set of headlights shot right by. Nobody stopped.

Then I saw a blinking red light and heard the sound of a siren behind me. For the first time in my life I was happy and excited to hear that sound! The state trooper got out of his car and said, "You know, Lady, that you're in danger out here alone on the freeway this late at night, don't you?"

I said, "Yes, sir, I know it."

He told me that it would take about five minutes to transfer some gas from his patrol car to mine, and invited me to sit in the squad car. I noticed that he was trembling and needed desperately to talk to someone.

He said, "I just came from an accident. A pregnant mother fell asleep, and her car veered off to the right and struck a cement culvert. I looked at the car with the one-third sheared off and thought, *Oh, oh, this is going to be one of those messy ones.* But the first thing I saw was a little two-year-old girl walking around with just one pulled tendon in her leg. What really unnerved me, though was that a Mrs. Beasley doll that was placed between the mother and daughter was decapitated by a piece of metal that came through the windshield, but the two of them were unharmed." He turned to me and asked, "Do you believe in God?"

I said, "Yes."

Then with deep emotion he said, "Do you think God was riding in the backseat of that car?"

I replied, "I think He may very well have been." Then I added, "Do you know that you're an answer to prayer too?"

He said, "Me? I'm an answer to prayer?"

Then I told him how I had prayed about every single pair of lights approaching my car that night.

This is only part of the story, and we must go back to Jacque for the end of it. "Evelyn, why did I feel an overwhelming urgency to pray for you last night? We were having a birthday party and I couldn't pray right then. But again God said, 'Jacque, pray for Evelyn.' So I gathered up the birthday wrappings, excused myself to take them out, and stood by the garbage cans, and prayed." Then she told me the exact time. Can you guess what time is was? Yes, it was exactly the time I had run out of gas on that freeway!

Is your communication system so open to God that you are available to pray any time of the day or night? When God sees a need down here on Planet Earth, can He say to you, "Wake up, wake up, I need you to pray for somebody"? Are you one of those with whom God can trust His burdens? Or are you like I was at one time, thinking you need eight hours of sleep or you'll collapse the next day?

"Pray without ceasing"—all day long, all night long. It's just a matter of having the communication system open between yourself and God so you can say at any time of day or night, "SOS, Lord." And He can say to you, "Knock, knock. There's a need down there. Will you please pray?"

For you to pray:

Dear Father, I want to be available to You, twenty-four hours a day. Teach me to open my communication with You and never shut it. Also help me to be available to others whenever they need me to pray.

THE VERTICAL DIMENSION OF PRAYER—
TO WHOM WE PRAY

Resist the devil and he will flee from you. Draw nigh to God, and He will draw nigh to you. James 4:7-8

An often overlooked but very important part of prayer is the drawing nigh to God. Before we are ready to start our intercessory prayers, we need to *wait* before God until we know we have established communication with Him. This is a time of silence when we are shutting out every other thought and distraction around us. This is not talking *to* God, just a complete mental drawing to Him; and then, as He promised, *He will draw nigh to us.*

DRAWING NIGH TAKES TIME

Drawing apart to God is important in groups as well as in private praying. It may be easier to do in our closets; but because of the hectic rush to arrive at a prayer meeting on time or because of the chatting after we've arrived, it is a must to pause for the seconds or minutes it takes to withdraw from all this and draw nigh to God. Often there seems to be embarrassment in a group if someone doesn't start praying audibly right away as we go to prayer—ready or not.

I remember way back in the "green chair" days struggling and struggling to draw nigh to God. I can recall how I would strain and wonder where He was. And it seemed as if my prayers were only reaching the ceiling. But through the years God has taught me many things—and I'm not in the struggling stage any more.

One thing I learned when I found it impossible to establish meaningful communication with God was that is wasn't His fault, it was mine. He is the same yesterday, today, and forever, but I am not. I let sins creep in that break my fellowship with Him, and frequently I must search my heart and confess those sins that are blocking communication between us.

I also learned the simple process of envisioning my God when approaching Him in prayer. The joy that floods my whole being as I find myself visualizing all God is—all His love, all His power, all His concern for me—defies description. What greater privilege could there be for a human being than to actually *draw nigh* to the omnipotent, omniscient God, high and lifted up on His throne in glory? This to me is the most precious part of my prayer time.

BE SURE IT'S GOD

Why do you suppose Christ taught His disciples, and us in turn, to pray, "Our Father who art in heaven"? Have you ever thought of that? Our God, capital *G*, is the only God in heaven, but there are other gods. "Thou shalt have no other gods before Me" (Exodus 20:3). If there were no other gods, our God would not have given Moses this commandment.

"The god of this world" is a title Paul gives Satan (2 Corinthians 4:4). In the explosion of the occult that is sweeping our nation, we are finding that even Christians—real Christians—are getting answers that are not from God. Christ spent one-fourth of His recorded ministry dealing with the enemy, and this is a warning to us to be constantly alert that we open our minds not to Satan but to God who is in heaven.

In a question and answer period following a lecture on the dangers of the occult at a church youth meeting, a man counselor raised his hand and asked, "Why is it that when I pray I get more answers from Satan than I do from God?" I didn't want to belittle that man before the students for whom he was responsible, but I had no choice. I looked at him, and I said as kindly as I could, "Sir, if you are getting more answers from Satan than you are from God, there's something drastically wrong with your prayer life."

Is it possible for even sincere Christians to unwittingly open themselves to suggestions from the enemy?

I know of five different pastors who claimed a voice said to them, "Divorce your wife," and each one promptly did. They said they thought it was the Lord speaking to them. But it was not surprising to learn that in every instance another woman was involved.

While flying over Canada, one pastor said to another, "I now know there is a life after death and I am preaching it from my pulpit."

"How do you know?" asked the surprised pastor sitting beside him.

"My stillborn baby is communicating with me. I

wasn't sure before, but I know now there is life after death!"

When I speak on the occult, I find to my horror that even Christian youth are experimenting with all sorts of occult practices. As I ask them what they do at slumber parties, their response is frightening. Many have crossed the thin line between parlor games and the occult. They are hearing voices during their séances, experiencing supernatural power, and getting answers in uncanny ways from Ouija boards.

After I had talked with one group of teenagers in a fine local church, a mother came to me and said, "I want to tell you that those kids had a Ouija board burning. My daughter is the ringleader of that junior high group in our church, and she came home from your meeting and said, 'Mother, playing with Ouija boards and all that stuff is an abomination to God. It says so in Deuteronomy 18.' "

Receiving supernatural answers through any form of divination or contact with mediums is not drawing nigh to God and is forbidden by Him (see Deuteronomy 18:9-14).

Halloween parties too seem to be changing in character these days. A friend of mine was having her hair done the week after Halloween. Her hairdresser said that every one of her customers who discussed attending any Halloween party said it turned out to be an attempt to draw nigh to spiritual beings other than God. What ever happened to bobbing for apples?

MEDITATION CAN BE DANGEROUS
Putting yourself into a state of passivity is a very

dangerous spiritual exercise, and one in which even true Christians are engaging. To open our minds and allow ourselves to be receptive to all the thoughts and suggestions which enter is a perilous business. We may think we are drawing nigh to God—but zing! There's Satan, and we are listening to *his* voice.

At a prayer seminar, a woman stepped up to me and said, "Do you know that I taught yoga and gave it up?"

I said, "Tell me, why did you give it up?"

"Well," she replied, "I suddenly realized that there I was in that room meditating with Buddhists, with Hindus, with people involved in every religion you can imagine. Sure, you sit there and you meditate and you get a feeling of peace and strength; but I've leaned that I get all the peace and strength I need from the Lord Jesus Christ, and I don't need yoga meditation. And God told me it's a sin for me to be meditating with those others who do not know the true God in heaven."

Oh, how foolish to put ourselves in such a vulnerable position! It does make a difference with whom we attempt to draw nigh to God. "What communion hath light with darkness?" (2 Corinthians 6:14)

Transcendental Meditation is a guise that Satan frequently uses today to infiltrate minds. It is being taught in many of our schools, libraries, YMCAs, YWCAs, and even in some churches.

While the president of a local woman's club and I were driving home together some seventy miles from a meeting, our conversation shifted to communicating. "You know," she said, "I communicate in the middle of the night. Do you?"

"Oh, yes, I communicate in the middle of the night," I replied.

She went on, "I know 'It' is out there, because I communicate with 'It.' "

I quickly changed the pronoun and said, "I know 'He' is out there. My God is out there."

She went on, "I don't know what it is I'm communicating with, but I know *something* is out there. Why don't you come to one of our meditation meetings? You can tell us how you communicate in the middle of the night, and we can tell you how we do." By that time I had an ill feeling in the pit of my stomach. I couldn't get out of that car fast enough!

Prayer is always directed from the pray-er up to God—who is in heaven. This is the vertical dimension of prayer. In the next chapter you will see how this dimension becomes a triangle when God reaches back down to earth with the answers to our prayers.

In Hebrews 11:6 we read that the faith that pleases God is two-faceted: believing that He is and believing that He is a rewarder of those who diligently seek Him. I wonder if before the occult explosion Christians really knew the full meaning of this. Have we concentrated so much on the fact that He is a rewarder that we have lost sight of *who* our God is—holy, high, and lifted up? We must draw nigh to *this* God—and then He will draw nigh to us.

Moses drew nigh to God when he "rose up early in the morning, and went up unto Mount Sinai" (Exodus 34:4,29-35). Do you remember what happened when he came down? The Children of Israel were afraid to come near him because the skin of his face shone! He had to put a veil over his face, it was so radiant. Wouldn't it be great if we could draw so close to God that we would become radiant? So close that others could tell by our very countenance that we had been with God? That we had learned the secret of His presence? That before bombarding Him with our requests, we had taken time to enter into His fellowship?

For you to do:

1. *Before starting to pray, in absolute silence practice drawing nigh to God. This may involve confessing some sin which God brings to your mind. If so, confess it, so that there is nothing between you and God in heaven.*
2. *Now draw nigh to Him. Wait in silence until you feel God is there.*
3. *Now pray, thanking God for who He is—whatever you want to say in adoration and praise for who He is—this God to whom you have just drawn nigh.*
4. *Now pray at least one request for some other person's need.*

THE HORIZONTAL DIMENSION OF PRAYER— RESULTS

But without faith it is impossible to please Him: for he that cometh to God must believe that He is, and that He is the rewarder of them that diligently seek Him.
Hebrews 11:6

ith the study of the horizontal dimension of prayer, we now come full circle. We have said that we cannot pray effectively when there is sin in our lives. We have described how to pray in God's will so that our prayers will be answered. We have spoken of the need to draw nigh to God, and to bask in the sunshine of His love because He never makes a mistake.

For what purpose have we taught about these prerequisites to prayer? Primarily, that we might become powerful, intercessory pray-ers. We are now back to the theme verse of chapter 1, "The effectual fervent prayer of a righteous [person] *availeth much*" (James 5:16, italics added).

The horizontal dimension of prayer is the visible result of our effective praying here on Planet Earth. But there can never be a horizontal dimension of prayer unless there is first the vertical dimension—that drawing nigh to God. The two are inseparable, standing as it were at the opposite points of the base of a triangle, with God at the top. The pray-er petitions God the Father, who receives the prayer, sifts it out according to His will, then reaches down to change people and circumstances on earth. The results we humans see represent the horizontal dimension of prayer.

UNITY

In chapter 1 you read many stories of what happens when women pray. Each was a visible result, on the horizontal level, of prayer that had ascended to God the Father, who in turn acted upon an individual or a set of circumstances here on earth. I also mentioned the tremendous unity that was experienced as members of the body of Christ prayed together. This unity is still happening.

Following the Day of Humiliation, Fasting, and Prayer for our country on April 30, 1974, I received telephone calls from several prayer seminar members. One woman said, "It was just beautiful in our group."

Another exclaimed, "Guess what? We finally got off the ground for the first time, really off the ground, and we're going to meet again next month, just as we did on April 30."

Another said, "We had the most beautiful experience. I helped our pastor organize the prayer meetings in our church. We used the Six S's and prayed in groups of four. It was a fantastic experience."

What else happened to many of us that day? We sensed deeply the humiliation for which we had prayed. With the continuing exposure of the Watergate affair, we knew that God was bringing us as individuals and our nation as a whole to the place of humiliation. And we felt a tremendous unity not as we studied together, or talked, or met as committee members, but as we prayed together. One definite horizontal result of prayer, then, is unity—in the church, in the home, in the community.

PRAYER TRANSCENDS MILES

Do you have loved ones who live a great distance from you? Perhaps a son or daughter who is away at school? Between my mother and me was the entire state of Wisconsin, and beyond that the vastness of Lake Michigan. Yet in prayer we both sensed a oneness that transcended the miles that separated us. God is not limited to space, as we are. He is able to reach down and give the unifying sense of His presence not only to people sitting beside us in the room but to individuals who are separated by continents. We proved this by an experiment in 1965.

After I had been praying with my two prayer partners Lorna and Sig every Thursday afternoon for almost a year, my husband and I went overseas to visit the mission fields. Before leaving we noted when we where scheduled to land in Addis Ababa, Ethiopia (where Sig's daughter Shirlee and her son-in-law Cliff were stationed). Our arrival would be just prior to the corresponding time that Lorna and Sig would be meeting for prayer in Rockford, though there would be an eight-hour difference on the clock. We calculated that if all the planes were on schedule and if everything went according to plan, we would be in Addis Ababa to pray with Sig's daughter and her husband at exactly the same time Sig was praying with Lorna in Rockford.

Having slept only two out of four nights en route, we arrived in Addis Ababa exhausted, but on schedule. All the guests went to bed except me. After the house was quiet, Cliff, Shirl, and I went to prayer in the living room. We had prayed for a short while when suddenly each of us had an overwhelming sense that no miles separated us and the two prayer partners back in Rockford. It was just as if they were right there praying with us. God had transcended all the miles across half the continent of the United States, the entire Atlantic Ocean, and most of the continent of Africa, and given to us a sense of oneness in His Spirit through prayer.

After we returned home, I was anxious to learn what had happened in Rockford that Thursday afternoon. Had they felt that oneness that transcends the miles? Sig said to me then, and she has repeated it over and over since, "Ev, I have never in all my years as a Christian been so aware of God and His power, so aware of His reality, as I was when I sensed that tremendous unity we had in Him, even though we were separated by thousands of miles." This too is the horizontal dimension of prayer, linking the prayers through our omnipresent God.

WE HAD NEVER MET

Closely related to the transcendence of miles is the bond created by prayer even among people who have never met. In 1968 one of the ladies in our prayer chain went to another state to purchase a poodle from a woman we know only as Joy. She had had major surgery involving the insertion of a plastic esophagus, and was having an extremely difficult pregnancy. It was no wonder that our prayer chain member came back and said, "Let's pray for Joy." We started, and week after week, month after month, we prayed for her.

One day after Joy delivered her baby, she told her husband that it was only because those women down there in Rockford were praying that she had the strength and the courage to get through her pregnancy. And that was not all—this dear woman accepted Christ as her personal Savior, and became the best missionary we ever had! Everyone who came to buy a poodle heard that she had found Christ, and was told about the women many miles away who had prayed and prayed for her physical and spiritual needs. To this day I haven't met Joy. It isn't likely that I will, for I don't think I'll ever buy a poodle. But God answered anyway!

On our prayer chain lists are many whom we have never met, but God knows who they are and where they are. He knows their needs. All we do is pray our requests—we don't pray answers—and with the mighty arm of His power, God reaches down to anyone anywhere on Planet Earth with his answers.

GOD IS THE REWARDER

Much happens when we pray. And answers come as we pray in faith believing. As I mentioned in the previous chapter, we come first of all believing that God is, and then believing unequivocally that He rewards those who seek Him. "But without faith it is impossible to please Him: for he that cometh to God must believe that He is, and that He is a rewarder of them that diligently seek Him" (Hebrews 11:6).

As we pray believingly, we see a fourth result in the horizontal dimension of prayer—*it is great in its working*. We are not dropping our prayers into a bottomless barrel. How do we know? One way is by the specific answers to specific requests. Early in our prayer ministry, we began to experience great answers to prayer. At the very first seminar in White Bear Lake, a woman handed me a request for our intercessory prayer time. It was for her sister to receive Christ. She said, "We've tried everything we know. We've talked to her; we've taken her to meetings where she's spurned invitation after invitation to receive Him. Please pray." Though they did not even know her name, 250 women zeroed in on that unsaved sister.

The next week the woman who had requested prayer stopped me before the seminar. "Do you know what? I took my sister to a Christian Women's Club luncheon right after the seminar last week, and she accepted Christ within two hours of your praying!" Those 250 pray-ers gave great praise during prayer time that day.

One morning we missed one of our prayer seminar steering committee members. Someone said, "She's taking her mother, who has TB, to the hospital."

Another woman suggested immediately, "Let's stop right now and pray."

Another steering committee member added, "But that isn't her mother's greatest need. Neither her mother nor her father knows Christ as Savior."

Instead of doing much planning that morning, we spent most of the time praying for the mother and father of our committee member. A couple of weeks after the seminar was over, still another member of the steering committee stopped me on the street and asked, "Ev, did you hear the good news? Within two weeks after the steering committee prayed, both the mother and father found Christ." In just two weeks! "The effectual fervent prayer of a righteous man availeth much" (James 5:16).

At a recent seminar session we prayed very definitely that a certain woman would find Christ. That very night she received Him as her Savior. In the same week we had another answer. A mother was called out of one of our seminars because her little boy had injured his leg at school and couldn't step on his foot. We promised to pray during the intercessory prayer time. When he was told that all those women had prayed for him, he said, "Then I must be okay." He threw away the ice pack, and went riding off on his bicycle!

God gave us another beautiful answer to prayer. We had learned that a young mother of twenty-three with two children had a cancerous growth on her brain. It was the type that had spread like the tentacles of an octopus, and her doctors gave her only a few weeks to live. All of us in the seminar went to prayer for this young mother, not just praying that she would be healed, but that God's will would be done in her life. In this instance, God chose to heal this young woman. A few weeks later, we learned that the tumor was shrinking rapidly and that there was not a sign of a cancerous cell in her whole body. The doctors had given her a normal life expectancy!

What happens when we pray? Things do happen. We do not drop our intercessory prayers into a bottomless barrel. We send them up to a Heavenly Father, who in His time, in His way, according to His will, answers them down here on Planet Earth.

REQUESTS CHANGE

Something else takes place in the horizontal dimension of prayer—we begin to see changes in our prayer requests. In 1968, when our prayer experimentation started, several in our denomination were trained in Washington, D.C. for the Crusade of the Americas. We returned to our homes all excited over the prospects of prayer and evangelism. I said to my husband, "We're going to pray for a year and then we're going to evangelize for a year."

He grinned and announced, "It'll never work."

Jolted, I asked, "Why not?"

He replied, "You show me somebody who's praying and I'll show you somebody who's evangelizing. A praying church is an evangelizing church."

He was right! Our objective had been to pray in 1968, and to evangelize in 1969. But when the time came for my report to our national committee in June 1969, I had to say, "The transition has already taken place."

We found that people who prayed automatically evangelized; they naturally shared their Christ with somebody else. With prayer chains praying for each of them, we developed thirty-five evangelism Bible studies in our church, in homes, offices, and in a high school, among women, couples, and young people. A Bible study group entirely composed of hippies was studying regularly as a result of Art Blessit's meeting that year. New converts had already become hosts, hostesses, and teachers for their evangelism Bible studies. We had participated in the distribution of Gospels to every home in our city.

In my 1969 report I said, "We are seeing our total church program becoming increasingly evangelistic, not superimposed by programs, but from within the hearts of the workers . . . . Our local church has been the greatest recipient of the blessings because we, as the pilot church, have put into practice the [prayer] ideas of the committee before they were passed on as being workable."

Are you concerned about outreach in your own life? In your church? When you have a praying life and a praying church, I guarantee you will have a life and a church with a vital outreach, because as we learn to pray, our prayer requests change.

It's interesting to go back and look at the careful notes I made in those months in 1968 when we first started to pray. I notice particularly that one had to have a broken leg or something equally serious to be included on our prayer lists! If we could see the need with our physical eyes—if it needed a bandage or a cast—we gave the request to our prayer chain. Otherwise it didn't get very much attention.

Gradually, though, things changed. As our spiritual eyes began to open, we saw spiritual needs and added these to our lists. God in heaven is concerned about physical needs. He expects us not only to pray about them but to put feet to our prayers, to bring in that casserole, or to help in any other way we can. But we aren't to stop there. We need to ask God to open our spiritual eyes that we might see the spiritual needs around us, especially in the lives of people who need to be transformed by Christ. This is the greatest need of every person on Planet Earth. But how can we share these prayer requests with others?

• Prayer Partners. After a banquet at which I had shared the horizontal blessings of a prayer ministry, a woman came to me with tears in her eyes. She said, "I'm overwhelmed; there's so much to remember. Where do I start?"

I told her that beyond her own personal praying, the place to start intercessory prayer is with one prayer partner. This is the best way I know. Find someone with whom you can share big things and little things. When you hurt or have a headache, when some little thing goes wrong, or when the whole world collapses around you, have one person you can trust absolutely, and upon whom you can call at any time. Find someone who will not betray your confidence, someone who is always ready to say whenever you give her a call, "I'll pray right now." Then, as you pray together, start praying for what God wants you to do for your church, family, and those in need. And then be open to those God would have pray with you.

• Church Lists. As our intercessory prayer develops on the horizontal level through private praying and prayer partners and prayer groups, we can proceed to church lists. One church in which we held a seminar encourages members of the congregation to fill out a form early in the Sunday morning service. It reads, "During our prayer time this morning, I would like my brothers and sisters in Christ to pray for . . . ." Following several blank spaces there is room for the signature of the person making the requests. These sheets are collected, and the pastor remembers the specific requests in his morning prayer.

The members of another congregation place their prayer requests on registration cards during the morning service. Later in the day these requests, along with items for praise, are listed on sheets which are distributed in the evening service. These are beautiful examples of members of the body of Christ praying for one another and bearing one another's burdens as members of Christ's family.

• Prayer Calendars. Prayer calendars represent another method of systematic prayer on the horizontal level. Usually two categories are covered—people and events. An individual may have a particular need on a certain day, or there may be a public meeting or an evangelistic effort which demands definite prayer. These requests may be on a local or a national level.

In 1968, in a circle of less than thirty women, we placed our names on a prayer calendar. Each woman prayed for a different woman each day so every person in that circle was prayed for daily. It was exciting. We heard women say, "I could feel you praying; my life was different when I knew that I was being supported and undergirded specifically by somebody in my circle."

There can be many variations in prayer calendars. Include missionaries, your pastor and church staff, youth ministries, and special projects. It is a great spiritual exercise.

Yes, when we started experimenting with all these methods of intercessory prayer in 1968, I wondered if anything would happen, if there would be any horizontal results. I'm not wondering anymore. I know from experience that the effectual, fervent prayer of a righteous person does avail much.

For you to do:

1. *Ask God to give you the next step He has for you in prayer—a prayer partner (ask for a specific name), a group He wants you to join or start, or a new method of prayer for your church, group, family, or club.*
2. *Wait in silence for Him to speak.*
3. *Promise Him you will start immediately whatever He is telling you to do.*

Telephone Prayer Chains

Be careful for nothing; but in everything by prayer and supplication with thanksgiving let your requests be made known unto God. Philippians 4:6

hat I missed most when I moved from Rockford, in the fall of 1970, was the 115 women who prayed for me on the telephone prayer chains. Every time I spoke, every time I was sick, every time there was a need in my family, these women prayed. I, of course, was not the only one for whom they interceded. There were hundreds of others whose physical and spiritual needs were brought before God.

For a long time after we moved to Minnesota, I kept a hot line going to Rockford with requests for the prayer chains. There were certainly pray-ers in my new home area, but I hadn't found them yet. I no longer need to dial Rockford as often, for there are many active prayer chains in our area now.

You don't have to be told that I believe strongly in prayer chains. They are very close to my heart since I depend almost entirely on the answers God gives when they go to prayer, and I act accordingly. When everyone is praying simultaneously for the same requests, there is really tremendous power in prayer. I know that great changes have taken place in my life because the prayer chains have prayed for me.

POWER OVER THE ENEMY

When I first started to speak against the occult, for example, I began to experience some horrible inner feelings. At times after speaking I was so filled with resentment and anger that I actually wanted to kick my car! Members of my family remarked that I was a different person when I spoke on that subject. Why was this so? Because I was intruding in Satan's realm. Then I took the advice of one of the leading Christian authorities on the subject of the occult, and formed a ten-member prayer chain from among the strongest pray-ers I knew.

The very next time I went out to speak on this subject, all those negative feelings had disappeared. Since that prayer chain was activated, I have had nothing but a victorious experience each time I have spoken against the occult.

PERSONAL NEEDS

Before leaving for meetings in another state, I asked several prayer chains to be praying at the exact hour when I would be appearing on a TV talk show. After I completed one speaking engagement at a Christian Women's Club luncheon, I was whisked crosstown to the TV studio to take part in the second half hour of the program. Arriving during the commercial between the two segments of the hour, I was not aware that a well-known false evangelist from Korea had just preceded me on the program. Had I known this, I would have been completely unnerved. Instead I chatted enthusiastically on the subject of prayer—how, when, and where God answers.

Friends who watched both half hours of that talk show told me the astounding difference there was between them. God had guarded me—because of all those simultaneous prayers.

I have a file folder bulging with recorded prayer requests and answers that were handled through our Rockford prayer chains. As I reviewed these in preparation for the writing of this book, I was overwhelmed at the number of times my name appears—on an average of four times a week! There are requests for my speaking engagements, for physical strength, and for help at times when I was ministering for Christ. Here's one example:

> "April 14: Pray for strength for Evelyn. She has the flu, and is scheduled to speak at Janesville tonight. The ladies want to learn about prayer chains and how to pray effectively."

> "April 15: Evelyn made the meeting. She had great praise. Many ladies were touched and eager to be changed."

It was always understood that they were to pray that God would make me well enough to go if it was His will that I be there.

You may feel that you could not have such a prominent place in the prayer concerns of a large group. Perhaps that is true. I have a wonderful privilege to be prayed for so much. Nevertheless, you can reap great benefits by finding just one or two prayer partners and praying regularly for and with one another. But remember, my prayer chains started with just eight members. Why don't you start one?

A TEACHING INSTRUMENT
FOR THE FAMILY

One exceptional benefit of being in a prayer chain is what it can do for your home. If you want to really teach prayer to your children, I know of no better way than prayer chain procedures.

As the children hear Mother calling through the prayer requests, and then watch as she bows her head immediately after putting down the receiver, they know that Mother believes in prayer. When the answer comes through they can hear her say, "Oh, that's great!" They watch her as she dials the next person on the prayer chain, and they listen as she says, "Praise God. He answered our prayer." They take note of her joy as she bows her head and thanks God for answering.

As prayer chain calls come into the home, the children and other members of the family can observe the progress of prayer, taking note of specific requests, specific answers, God's timing, and the flow of praise.

For our family this has been one of the greatest teaching instruments through all the years of bringing up our children. They believe so much in prayer chains that both our daughters, when they were out of town, have spent their own money to call long distance with requests. Now our son, Kurt, the only child still living at home, every once in awhile comes out with, "I think it's time to call the prayer chain!"

Once while Kurt and I were painting the ceiling

of our sun porch, the telephone rang, but I wasn't in any particular hurry to answer—I was up a ladder with the paint dripping down my arms! Our daughter Nancy picked up the kitchen phone, and in a few seconds she called in, "Never mind, Mother, it's *just* another answer to prayer."

On her wedding day, Nancy herself was a subject for prayer. The note from my file reads: "June 8—6:30 P.M. Chris called the prayer chain with a specific request: 'Pray for Nancy who is vomiting and has diarrhea. Pray for God's divine healing as she will be married at 7:30 tonight.' "

The entry on June 9 reads: "Nancy was a bit queasy in the tummy, but came through in fine shape for the wedding!"

In Rockford we had an amusing illustration of the way children are impressed by the prayer chains. Our church children's worker, Gail, was teaching prayer to a group of fifth- and sixth-graders. While meeting one Saturday, Gail said to the youngsters, "Would you please pray for the pastor's wife? She's speaking in Chicago today."

Just then a little boy raised his hand and said, "Never mind. You know that thing—that prayer chain thing? They've already prayed. It's all done."

Prayer chains provide a wonderful method of teaching complete confidence in answered prayer, and in the God who answers prayer. Let your children hear these specific answers that are reported over your telephone. It will do something for your entire family.

Whole families are involved in the ministry of

prayer chains. I remember one Sunday in Rockford, a well-known Gospel singer and his family were visiting his parents. He is paralyzed from the waist down, and on that particular day his urinary tract stopped functioning. By 6 P.M. the family was quite alarmed and called the emergency room.

As they were ready to leave for the hospital, his mom said, "Let's try the prayer chain first." At 6:20, when everybody was scurrying around getting ready for the evening church service, the prayer chains were activated. The request could not have come at a better time; everybody was home. Members of whole families stopped what they were doing and prayed for him. Later his mother said, "A very amazing thing happened. While the prayer chains were praying, suddenly, it was as though an electric shock whizzed right through our house—and through my son's body. His whole system started to function normally once again."

CHURCH FAMILIES TOO

Another beautiful illustration of family involvement was the result of a request dated Sunday, March 23: "Please pray for Becky. She has started labor pains. The baby is not due for seven or eight weeks." (Becky is the one mentioned in an earlier chapter, whose only child was lost through a crib death.) That morning, before Sunday School, 120 homes received this specific request through the prayer chains. Mothers, fathers, and children all stopped to pray.

Later, the burden was shared in every department of the Sunday School and the whole church family joined in prayer for Becky. The notation made on Monday, March 24, reads: "Pray for Becky, and especially her 3 lb., 8 oz. daughter." On Tuesday, March 25, the request was urgent: "Becky's baby has developed lung complications. Pray that God's strength will sustain Becky and Eddie, that the God who never makes a mistake will do what is best." God worked in a wonderful way.

Becky and I belonged to the same circle in our church. Every month when she brought that healthy, happy little "answer to prayer" to our meetings and set her on a blanket in the middle of the floor, she gave us a precious reminder of God's ability to answer prayer!

FELT IN HOSPITALS

Many prayer chain requests are for those who are confined in hospitals. I have one note in my folder which reads: "Alice went to see Inez, who remarked, 'Your friends must be really praying. God was so near to me, and I'm not afraid anymore.' Her tests show a malignancy, and the nurses and her roommates can't understand the change in her attitude. She tells them God did it, and she's not afraid anymore."

There was also praise from Florence: "I'm so thankful God took me through this last experience. I was never more conscious that He was near. Each day I felt upheld by your prayers."

As we received thank-you notes and telephone calls from patients for whom we prayed, most of them said, "I could feel you praying."

BIBLE STUDY GROUPS

Some of the most exciting answers to our prayer chain praying have come out of Bible study groups. For example, there was Lynn who had threatened to break up our meeting the first time she attended one of my Bible studies. She stood on her head, showing us how she had learned to meditate in her search for answers to life. Our prayer chains were already praying for her, and Lynn found Christ when she attended the Bible study the second time. After receiving Him she said to me, "I want to be on the prayer chain that prayed for me." Immediately she requested prayer for her friend Sandy to find Christ. Then came the day when she called full of excitement, "Sandy just accepted Christ!" After a long pause, she said, "Now I'll have to find somebody else to put on the prayer chain."

Do you believe that thoroughly in prayer? Lynn does.

Among my notes, I have a request dated March 19, pertaining to Friendship Bible Coffees: "Lee would like us to pray for the seven Bible studies this morning and others this afternoon. Pray especially that the Holy Spirit will convict of the need for salvation." The answer: "Four found Christ today!" One of the requests our prayer chains honored every day was to pray specifically for those attending the Bible studies.

SEMINARS

Recently I received a call from the chairman of a

previous prayer seminar that illustrates the way prayer chains grow out of these sessions. She said, "This is the week you're going to teach prayer chains in your present five-week seminar, isn't it?" I told her it was. Then she went on, "Well, I'm leaving for California, but I want you to know what we have done in our area. We have just started six prayer chains, and we have almost enough people to form a seventh. We have three morning chains, an evening chain, and an emergency chain that operates around the clock. Both men and women take part in this one. And we average three to nine requests per day on those prayer chains."

I then asked, "What's happening?"

She answered, "We're taking requests for physical and spiritual problems, and from those who are having difficulties in their homes, and we're seeing problems cleared up with beautiful answers to prayer. This is the most exciting thing that has come out of our prayer seminar. We're finding a unity among people from all the different churches that are represented on our prayer chains, and we feel this is a real service to the Lord."

The chairwoman of our retreat at Forest Home in California wrote, "Prayer chains are spreading up all around now—men's, women's, and even children's prayer chains!" Prayer chains are not just for women. It's exciting to see everyone in a church involved— the pastor, members of the various boards, the Sunday School—everybody. A host pastor at one of our prayer seminars started an all-men's prayer chain with the challenge to the men in one of his church groups. "You know," he said, "there are certain things I cannot give to women to pray about. I need some men volunteers." He got them—100 percent!

A national youth speaker called me long distance and said, "I just listened to your prayer tapes while I was driving from Michigan to Pennsylvania. Now I feel that I wouldn't dare go through these fourteen speaking engagements, where I'll be bringing messages against the occult, without prayer." We prayed, and when I next heard from him, he wrote, "I could feel you praying and I never had such freedom, such attentiveness, and discipline in the school where I spoke."

THE CHAIRMAN

In Rockford we had ten prayer chains with ten or so persons on each chain. Because we wanted to have as many people as possible praying simultaneously, our chairman, after receiving the calls and recording the requests verbatim, called person number one on all ten of the prayer chains, and in fifteen minutes 115 people were praying.

Incoming prayer requests may come from any source, but it's important that only the bare essentials be communicated in the request. A discerning chairman will sense when something is too personal, and will ask, "Have you checked with the person for whom you're requesting prayer?" As I look over the recorded requests in my folder I am amazed at the spiritual insight of our chairman and the careful wording she used in the prayer requests. For years she had helped me with housework in the parsonage, and we had spent many hours there in prayer together. But then came the day when after much surgery, she could no longer do housework and felt that God was calling her to be our prayer chain chairman.

When she accepted the position, she stood up in our women's meeting and said, "I thank God for all the pain and the surgery, for He has shown me that there's something much greater that I can do for Evelyn than ironing and baking cookies."

NO GOSSIPING

A testimony by one of our prayer recipients attests to the strong commitment of our prayer chain members. It happened that the woman who was my Bible study hostess for three years had a daughter who had left home and strayed far from Christ. Through her broken marriage, a divorce, and her remarriage, our prayer chains kept praying for this dear girl, and then for her new mate.

One day, while they were traveling in the East, this couple stepped out of their car, knelt in a parking lot, and without any human intervention, both accepted Christ as their personal Savior. When they came back to our church in Rockford, the husband gave a testimony during a Sunday morning service. He said, "My wife and I owe our eternal salvation to the prayer chains of this church."

When they went to study at a Christian college, the wife related her experience to a group of faculty wives, "The thing that really astounded me after I came back home was that not one person of the 115 on those telephone prayer chains gossiped. They all knew I had been married and divorced, and that this was my second husband, but no one else in the church knew about it."

That is the way it should be.

It's possible that some may find it difficult to keep juicy information confidential. If such is the case, they could call the chairman and say, "I would like my name removed from the prayer chains." This hasn't happened yet in our experience, but someday it might!

We have found that it is a great source of strength for prayer chain members to sign the list of rules governing chain procedures at one time, while they are all together. In this way it is not a commitment to a person, or to a prayer chain chairman, but it is a commitment to God.

Our basic rules are few and simple. Members promise to pray *immediately* when receiving the requests by telephone. They also promise to pass on the request immediately to the next person in the prayer chain. They are not to delete anything or add anything to the request. And they are to keep it confidential—no gossiping.

THE STRONGEST LINK

Ordinary chains are as weak as their weakest link, but a prayer chain is as strong as its strongest link. Why is this so? Because every single link in a prayer chain, every member, is united from here on earth to God in heaven. The weak and the strong are praying simultaneously to God the Father, and we see the dramatic, exciting results here on Planet Earth.

In January 1968, we started our first prayer chain with 8 gripers, and in just a few months we had 66 pray-ers. From March to December, these 66 pray-ers prayed for 508 requests which multiplied to 33,528 prayers to God the Father, who sent back as many answers. Multiply your prayers on a chain and watch exciting things happen!

A CHAIN REACTION

Prayer chains have a peculiar and wonderful way of linking people together. We found this out when our Jan made a long distance telephone call from college to our prayer chairman in Rockford— 325 miles away. The chain reaction started with her request on Tuesday, May 12, 1970: "Pray for God to be with and help the wife of a professor at Bethel [Jan's chemistry teacher]. She has a serious back problem and was to have had immediate surgery, but they just found out that she is pregnant. She has to be in bed much of the time and cannot take many pain pills since they might hurt the baby." Periodically after that we prayed for Sharon.

Two years later, after moving from Rockford, I was having my first Bible study class in St. Paul, when a young mother with a toddler in tow introduced herself to me in the church parking lot: "I'm Sharon," she said.

"Are you *the* Sharon for whom our prayer chains prayed when our Jan was so concerned about her chemistry professor's wife?" I asked.

As she grinned and nodded, her girlfriend spoke up, "Oh Sharon, *that's why* you had such an easy delivery!"

Not long after that I was almost 2,000 miles away teaching the Six S's and telephone prayer chains at a women's retreat at Forest Home in California. I read some illustrations of prayer chain requests directly from the bulging file folder—my most powerful teaching tool! As I read the request Jan had phoned in from Bethel in 1970, a woman sitting in the back of the auditorium waved her hand to get my attention. She said, "I have an urgent request from Sharon's mother-in-law. She just found out today that Sharon's husband's brother has an extremely serious brain tumor." God gave to that roomful of women a tremendous sense of urgency as we broke into groups of four to practice and experience the reality of "praying in one accord."

Returning to St. Paul, I immediately placed this pressing request with the faculty wives' prayer chain which we had recently started. Through the long, difficult illness and death of his brother, we continued to pray for this professor's need. And now, who do you think has been the telephone prayer chairman of this faculty wives' prayer chain for the past two years? Yes, Sharon.

Sharon was also one of those chosen to be on my first personal prayer chain in the Twin Cities. The chain is still active, and this last year the other members and I prayed for Sharon through another difficult pregnancy, and through the baby's late arrival (timed by God after the brother's out-of-state funeral). Next we prayed for the new baby's surgery. And we continued to pray about Sharon's back problem—

for which we started prayer four and one-half years earlier in Rockford! Sharon finally had that surgery, and mother and baby are now doing beautifully.

Yes, telephone prayer chains (as all forms of prayer) have a unique way of joining the human links together on a horizontal plane here on earth. But the marvel of it is that each individual is directly connected to the source of power of the whole universe, who is up in heaven—God Himself!

"Lord, teach me to pray! Amen."